University of Michigan Business School Management Series

INNOVATIVE SOLUTIONS TO THE PRESSING PROBLEMS OF BUSINESS

The mission of the University of Michigan Business School Management Series is to provide accessible, practical, and cutting-edge solutions to the most critical challenges facing business-people today. The UMBS Management Series provides concepts and tools for people who seek to make a significant difference in their organizations. Drawing on the research and experience of faculty at the University of Michigan Business School, the books are written to stretch thinking while providing practical, focused, and innovative solutions to the pressing problems of business.

Executive Summary

The ability to achieve our goals, fulfill our missions, and make our contributions to the world depends as much on our *social capital* (the resources available in and through personal and business networks) as it does on our *human capital* (knowledge, expertise, and experience). People who build the right networks get the resources they need when they need them—entrepreneurs secure venture capital, investors find new business opportunities, job seekers locate good jobs, salespeople find new customers, managers boost their influence and effectiveness, business leaders tap the competitive advantage of human resources by building social capital as an organizational competence.

Research also shows a direct link between social capital and the quality, purpose, and meaning of life. Good networks improve happiness, health, and even longevity. Building networks improves our personal lives as it contributes to the world by making it a more connected place.

This book guides you through the process of evaluating, building, and using social capital. After introducing the subject of social capital (Chapter One), it shows you how to use sociometric techniques to analyze the state and quality of your personal and business networks (Chapter Two), boost your access to resources by making your networks more entrepreneurial through more than twenty proven practices used by free agents and members of organizations (Chapter Three), and use social capital ethically and invoke the power of reciprocity by deploying your social capital in service to others (Chapter Four). Finally, it turns to the level of the organization, focusing on ten practices that entrepreneurs, business owners, managers, executives, and business leaders can use to build social capital as an organizational competence (Chapter Five).

Achieving Success Through Social Capital

Tapping the Hidden Resources in Your Personal and Business Networks

Wayne Baker

JOSSEY-BASS
A Wiley Company
San Francisco

Jossey-Bass books and products are available through most bookstores. To contact Jossey-Bass directly, call (888) 378-2537, fax to (800) 605-2665, or visit our website at www.josseybass.com.

Substantial discounts on bulk quantities of Jossey-Bass books are available to corporations, professional associations, and other organizations. For details and discount information, contact the special sales department at Jossey-Bass.

TCF Manufactured in the United States of America on Lyons Falls Turin Book. This paper is acid-free and 100 percent totally chlorine-free.

Library of Congress Cataloging-in-Publication Data

Baker, Wayne E.
     Achieving success through social capital : tapping the hidden resources in your personal and business networks / Wayne Baker.— 1st ed.
          p. cm. — (University of Michigan Business School management series)
     ISBN 0-7879-5309-1 (acid-free paper)
     1. Business networks. 2. Social networks. 3. Human capital.
4. Success in business. I. Title. II. Series.
     HD69.S8 B349 2000
     650.1—dc21   00-009554

FIRST EDITION
HB Printing   10 9 8 7 6 5 4 3 2 1

Contents

Foreword

Welcome to the University of Michigan Business School Management Series. The books in this series address the most urgent problems facing business today. The series is part of a larger initiative at the University of Michigan Business School (UMBS) that ties together a range of efforts to create and share knowledge through conferences, survey research, interactive and distance training, print publications, and new media.

It is just this type of broad-based initiative that sparked my love affair with UMBS in 1984. From the day I arrived I was enamored with the quality of the research, the quality of the MBA program, and the quality of the Executive Education Center. Here was a business school committed to new lines of research, new ways of teaching, and the practical application of ideas. It was a place where innovative thinking could result in tangible outcomes.

The UMBS Management Series is one very important outcome, and it has an interesting history. It turns out that every year five thousand participants in our executive program fill out a marketing survey in which they write statements indicating the most important problems they face. One day Lucy Chin, one of our administrators, handed me a document containing all these statements. A content analysis of the data resulted in a list of forty-five pressing problems. The topics ranged from growing a company to managing personal stress. The list covered a wide territory, and I started to see its potential. People in organizations tend to be driven by a very traditional set of problems, but the solutions evolve. I went to my friends at Jossey-Bass to discuss a publishing project. The discussion eventually grew into the University of Michigan Business School Management Series— Innovative Solutions to the Pressing Problems of Business.

The books are independent of each other, but collectively they create a comprehensive set of management tools that cut across all the functional areas of business—from strategy to human resources to finance, accounting, and operations. They draw on the interdisciplinary research of the Michigan faculty. Yet each book is written so a serious manager can read it quickly and act immediately. I think you will find that they are books that will make a significant difference to you and your organization.

Robert E. Quinn, Consulting Editor
M.E. Tracy Distinguished Professor
University of Michigan Business School

Preface

When my colleague Bob Quinn approached me with his idea for the UMBS Management Series, I immediately proposed this book on social capital. In the years since I wrote my first book on the topic, *Networking Smart: How to Build Relationships for Personal and Organizational Success* (1994), so much has changed that the message of social capital is more important than ever before, and therefore I was delighted to have the opportunity to write a new book about it.

What has changed? First, it is now clear that society is shifting to a new stage of development—the network society. This change shows itself at many levels: the emergence of global business networks; the widespread adoption of the network organizational design, where flexible internal networks replace rigid functional silos, and complex external networks of alliances and partnerships replace traditional arm's-length relationships between organizations; the end of lifelong employment with one company and the rise of free agency; and the decline of traditional, well-defined career paths and their replacement with zigzag, self-designed careers woven across companies and industries. Perhaps most obviously, it shows itself in the skyrocketing use of electronic network technologies, such as e-mail, groupware, the Internet, and the Web, with the emergence of computer-supported cooperative work, cyberspace communities, hard-wired neighborhoods, and so on. We live and work in networks, now more than ever before, and so building and using social capital are more essential skills now than ever before.

Second, there is a lot more information available about networks and social capital. The scientific study of networks, conducted by a worldwide community of sociologists, social psychologists, organizational scholars, medical researchers, economists, and political scientists, has grown exponentially. Social scientists now know more than ever before about how to measure social capital, build it, and use it. Research today establishes a clear link between social capital and valued personal and business benefits. Given the knowledge explosion, a new book is required to capture this new scientific knowledge, add it to the foundation of earlier research, and make it available for the benefit of individuals and organizations in the business world.

Third, there is a growing gap between the need for social capital in a network society and the ability of individuals and organizations to build and use it. Evidence of this gap shows itself in many places. For example, Edward M. Hallowell, M.D., of the Harvard Medical School observes the disappearance in modern life of "human moments"—genuine face-to-face interactions. In *Connect*, he prescribes small acts of compassion and face-to-face conversation to supplement the modern diet of electronic, at-a-distance communication.[1] The evolution of society to a new stage of development is not painless. Many of the pressing problems in modern organizations are "people" problems—corrosive political climates, the challenge of multiple accountabilities, overwork in demanding environments, underemployed human resources, cultural misunderstandings in global companies, and chaotic role movements—to name just a few.[2] My consulting and research over the years has shown repeatedly that individuals and organizations struggle to learn how to succeed in the network society. And my experience continuously reveals the great benefits that accrue from developing social capital in business, as well as the great costs borne by those who don't.

This book is a practical, step-by-step guide to assessing your social capital, building your social capital, and using your social capital. It stands on a solid foundation of research, but the focus throughout is pragmatic and down-to-earth. The notes at the end of the book are evidence of this scientific basis. I provide these notes for both the curious and the skeptical—but you don't have to look at them to get the full benefit of this book.

■ Audience

Who will benefit from working though this book? Let me answer that question with a partial list of those who *have* benefited, based on using this book's material in my social capital workshops, consulting work, assessments, and executive education, MBA, and undergraduate business courses: entrepreneurs looking for venture capital; business-government-education alliances seeking to build local networks of entrepreneurs and venture capitalists; job hunters looking for new jobs; people making major and minor career transitions; salespeople looking to expand their customer networks; MBA students preparing to run small companies or thrive in big ones; undergraduate business students preparing for their first professional jobs; small business owners striving to build virtual companies; managers of big organizations learning to thrive in the network organization; human resources trainers and organizational development consultants looking to add powerful new concepts and tools to their repertories; leaders of big and midsized companies seeking new models of leadership, along with frameworks, proven practices, and tools to tap the competitive advantage of "people power" by building social capital as an organizational competence.

I'd like to conclude this Preface with a personal reason for writing this book. I saw in the UMBS Management Series an opportunity to further the fulfillment of my mission. My mission can be stated in one sentence, and not even a complete one at that: "To contribute to the theory and practice of a more humane society." My definition of "a more humane society" is one in which we see ourselves as members of a vast network of interdependent connections, where we take each other's welfare into account and build relationships of mutual respect, honor, and understanding, and where we contribute to each other's human development and the fulfillment of each other's hopes and aspirations. I attempt to fulfill the "theory" part of my mission by continued scholarly research on networks and social capital. Like many academics, I publish esoteric articles in inaccessible scholarly journals. But I try to translate these ideas and put them into practice. Many colleagues in my home discipline of sociology frown on such activities, but I believe that the proper role of the intellectual is to conduct research on important topics and to make the world a better place by putting these ideas into practice. I try to fulfill the "practice" part of my mission by public speaking, by teaching in a business school, by consulting, and by writing books like this one.

■ Acknowledgments

I thank Bob Quinn for the grand opportunities created by the UMBS Management Series, and for its energizing effect on our faculty. I acknowledge the Jossey-Bass team, especially Cedric Crocker and Byron Schneider, who are full partners in our joint venture. I am particularly grateful to John Bergez of Bergez & Woodward, who showed me that the fine art of developmental editing still lives.

I thank the many colleagues, friends, students, and acquaintances who shared their personal stories, observations, and experiences about social capital. Their examples grace these pages: John Agno, Aundrea Almond-Wallace, Lindsay Armishaw, Richard Borer, Lynne Cannon, Tom Caprel, Bret Chennault, John Clendenin, Jason Cohen, Michael Crescenzi, Murray Cruickshank, Jerry Davis, Linda Dorosh, Jane Dutton, Betsy Egan, Diana Economy, Rob Faulkner, Chuck Gremel, Bill Kessor, Eric Monteiro, Judy Olson, Peter Ringrose, Jeff Sanborn, Anjali Sastry, John Tropman, Ed Vielmetti, Jim Walsh, Stephanie Wargo, Susie Wiley, Chris Workman, Martha Young, Sandra Xenakis, and Roberta Zald.

As has become my custom, I've saved the most important acknowledgement for last. I acknowledge with love and gratitude my wife, Cheryl, my partner in all senses of the word. Thank you for all you have taught me about building relationships.

May 2000   Wayne Baker
Ann Arbor, Michigan

With love to my wife and friend, Cheryl

What Is Social Capital, and Why Should You Care About It?

This book is a guide to *social capital*—what it is, how to evaluate it, how to build it and use it. This chapter defines social capital and explains why social capital is so important. "Social capital" refers to the resources available in and through personal and business networks. These resources include information, ideas, leads, business opportunities, financial capital, power and influence, emotional support, even goodwill, trust, and cooperation. The "social" in social capital emphasizes that these resources are not personal assets; no single person owns them. The resources reside in networks of relationships. If you think of human capital as *what* you know (the sum of your own knowledge, skills, and experience), then access to social capital depends on *who* you know—the size, quality, and diversity of your personal and business networks. But beyond that, social capital also depends on who you *don't* know, if you are indirectly connected to them via your networks.

"Capital" emphasizes that social capital, like human capital or financial capital, is productive: It enables us to create value, get things done, achieve our goals, fulfill our missions in life, and make our contributions to the world. But saying that social capital is "productive" is an understatement: No one can be successful—or even survive—without it. But many people believe they should be able to get along without social capital; they mistake "going it alone" as the prescription for success. Others pretend to thrive without social capital, using it secretly as if it were improper or even unethical.

These beliefs and attitudes are rooted in the myth of *individualism:* the cultural belief that everyone succeeds or fails on the basis of individual efforts and abilities. This myth is so powerful—and such an obstacle to achieving success through social capital—that I'll address it head on in the first section of this chapter. Despite the myth of individualism, social capital is an essential part of achieving personal success, business success, and even a happy and satisfying life. Next, I build a business case for social capital—the scientifically proven benefits of relationships for people, groups, and firms in the world of business. And I'll even go beyond the business case to consider the links between networks and the greater concerns of life—health, longer life, and a sense of meaning, fulfillment, and the ability to contribute to the world.

I'll conclude the chapter with a thorny issue: the ethics of using social capital. These thorns are imaginary. We can't *avoid* managing relationships; our only choice is *how* we manage them. Managing our networks consciously is an ethical duty—and the prescription for personal and business success.

■ Reconsidering Success: The Myth of Individualism

What does it take to be successful—to achieve career and life goals? When I pose this question to my consulting clients, audiences, and students, I get a variety of answers. The source of success is natural talent, intelligence, education, or effort. It might even be sheer luck. Whatever the source, the unspoken assumption behind these answers is always the same: Success is an individual matter. Every person succeeds or fails on the basis of his or her own individual efforts and abilities. This assumption is so powerful that when I suggest an alternative view—success depends on our relationships with others as much as it does on ourselves—the usual reaction I get is denial. This reaction gets stronger when I suggest that pay, promotion, and accomplishments are largely determined by the structure and composition of one's personal and business networks. And the last straw is my suggestion that it is our ethical duty to deliberately manage relationships—and that anyone who doesn't is unethical.

Psychologists would say that the "denial response" comes from the need to maintain a positive self-image. Denial of the role of relationships, for example, preserves the self-enhancing illusion that we are masters of our own fates: we get all the credit for our successes. This psychological response might be real, but the reason for denial is much deeper. Every society is organized around "cultural myths" that give meaning and purpose to life. One prevalent in this culture is the fiction that success is an individual matter. To suggest that one's fate depends on relationships runs counter to one of the dearest American values: individualism. Individualism is one of the nation's founding principles; Americans are born into a culture that teaches and celebrates independence, self-reliance, self-sufficiency, self-interest, and self-determination. The American hero is the rugged individualist. For example, everyone knows (and is inspired by) Horatio Alger tales—rags-to-riches stories of individuals who achieve great success on the strength of their own efforts. Americans revere the go-it-alone mentality, the frontier spirit, the lone wolf thriving without others. This myth has many names but the message is always the same: *Success is an individual enterprise.* To suggest otherwise is almost un-American.

But that is my message—individualism is a myth. James Coleman, one of the most influential social scientists of the last fifty years, called individualism "a broadly perpetrated fiction in modern society." "This fiction is that society consists of a set of independent individuals, each of whom acts to achieve goals that are independently arrived at, and that the functioning of the social system consists of the combination of these actions of independent individuals."[1] This fiction or myth gets in the way of understanding how the world actually works. And in doing so it lowers our chances of success, depresses our pay, limits our promotions, decreases the value we create, reduces our ability to get things done, and even jeopardizes our health, happiness, and welfare. And it closes off all the great possibilities of life. By understanding the role of relationships, however, we can tap hidden resources that will enable us to be much more successful in all areas of our lives—work, family, and community.

Everyone's first task is to "unlearn" the lessons of individual achievement.[2] The place to start is by considering the role of networks in the "individual" attributes people love to claim: natural talent, intelligence, education, effort, and luck.

Natural Talent

Physical and mental talents depend on genes, but inherited abilities explain only part of a person's performance; the environment is as important—if not more so.[3] Natural talent is expressed and developed via relationships with others. Why, for example, did the U.S. women's soccer team win the World Cup in 1999?

The team included highly talented individuals. But their individual talents had been spotted, honed, and nurtured by scores of coaches, teachers, and trainers. The players mastered their skills through many years of organized team play. Several members of the U.S. team had played together for years (including at the Olympic Games). They had the good fortune to be born at a time when a soccer infrastructure existed that provided opportunities to play and develop. America never had a world-class team before simply because the infrastructure to develop one didn't exist—not because the nation lacked young women with natural talents for playing world-class soccer.

But soccer is a *team* sport, you might object, and so of course individual success is interrelated with the performances of others. What about an individual sport, like golf? Consider the visual interplay between Sergio Garcia, the young pro golfer from Spain, and top-ranked Tiger Woods on the last few holes of the 1999 PGA Championship at Medinah, Illinois. Garcia's dashing play (including an eyes-closed chop that scooped the ball out of exposed tree roots) whittled Woods's lead to nothing. Woods (and the commentators) didn't miss the bold, challenging look Garcia cast at him from one hole to the next. Woods used this challenge to rally, rescue his lead, and win the tournament. Garcia finished second, right on Woods's heels.

Think of one of your gifts of natural talent. Who helped to nurture it? What role did your relationships with family, friends, coaches, teachers, trainers, teammates, and others play in the discovery, development, and expression of your natural talent?

Intelligence

Intelligence, like natural talent, depends on inherited genes. But again, that's only part of the story. " At one time, it was believed that intelligence was fixed—that we are stuck forever with whatever level of intelligence we may have at birth," notes Yale psychologist Robert Sternberg. "Today, many and perhaps most researchers in the field of intelligence believe that it is malleable—that it can be shaped and even increased through various kinds of interventions."[4] The home environment, availability and quality of schooling, and other factors play major roles. Early childhood interventions such as Head Start raise intelligence and achievement scores.[5] A nurturing and stimulating preschool home environment (interactive caregivers, organized and varied activities, appropriate play materials, and so on) matters more than other factors, such as socioeconomic conditions. Isolation, neglect, and deprivation crush intelligence—to the point of mental retardation.[6]

The malleability of intelligence illustrates the difference between the brain and the mind: Everyone is born with a physical *brain;* but a human *mind* develops only through relationships. Indeed, the human brain evolved neurologically in response to an increasingly complex social environment, developing a specialized organic ("hardwired") ability to perceive social events and human interactions. The mind arises in a social context that defines its form and figure; consciousness, self-awareness, awareness of others as mental selves, and the emotions are all relational.[7] Neuroscientists call this the "social mind" to emphasize that "the mind is communal in its very nature: It cannot be derived from any single brain in isolation."[8] Indeed, ongoing human contacts are necessary for physiological and emotional well-being.[9]

Education

The fact that you and I are communicating through the written word is testimony to the many relationships involved in human education. We learn language through observation of and interaction with others. If I had been born in Beijing, for example, I would be writing in Baihua, the modern written vernacular of standard Mandarin. Literacy is a function mainly of educational opportunities. We read and write because others—parents, relatives, teachers, tutors, older siblings or friends—taught us how. Education is an important component of "human capital." Investing in one's human capital by going to college, earning advanced degrees, and making learning a lifelong process is a critical element of success. But making this personal investment is possible only through relationships with others; indeed, social capital facilitates the creation of human capital. For example, a high school student is much more likely to stay in school if both parents are present, the student has few siblings (and so the parents can concentrate their attention and other resources), the parents expect their child to attend college, and the family doesn't move often (residential stability facilitates relationships between the student's parents and teachers and the parents of schoolmates, and between the student and teachers and other adults in the community).[10]

Effort

Everyone knows people who succeed even though they aren't the most talented, the cleverest, or the best educated. They simply never give up. Effort is clearly related to success, but is it a purely individual trait? Clearly, there are natural variations in physical and mental energy. But the fields of organizational behavior and psychology demonstrate conclusively that the amount of effort expended varies tremendously with the social context. Fast runners prefer to compete against other fast runners (called a "fast field") because it elevates their individual performance. Some work settings are motivating; others are demotivating. A person is more likely to work harder in a high-productivity workplace than in a low-productivity workplace. Good managers know how to motivate people by setting explicit and specific goals ("do your best" doesn't bring forth as much effort as a specific target), providing timely and useful feedback, and by artfully using rewards and incentives. They understand that the social environment greatly influences effort.

Even the goals we choose are defined by the culture in which we live. The goal of monetary success, for example, is central in American society.[11] Yet this devotion to making money is unprecedented in history. Up until a few hundred years ago, the continuous pursuit of profit for its own sake was a sin, charging any interest on a loan was illegitimate (usury), and a concept such as maximizing shareholder value would have been considered evil.[12] The goals we choose are influenced by those around us. As mentioned earlier, a student whose parents expect their child to attend college is more likely to go to college than one whose parents regard college as unnecessary or inappropriate. A teacher or mentor may encourage us to set higher goals than we would otherwise; a role model inspires us to achieve them.

Luck

Chance and happenstance are ingredients of success. For example, accidental discovery is responsible for a host of scientific and technical breakthroughs: penicillin, insulin, dynamite, Teflon, Post-it notes, plastics, and many others. Some people seem to have a knack for being in the right place at the right time. Yet this kind of luck is not accidental; it is cultivated. Studies show that lucky people increase their chances of being in the right place at the right time by building a "spiderweb structure" of relationships that catches lots of different bits and pieces of information.[13] They increase the chances of beneficial accidental encounters by living in a zigzag, not a straight line. Creativity can be managed. For example, creative types boost their luck by bouncing their ideas off others, learning from others, helping others, and so on. Some science labs have even changed the physical configuration of their labs and offices to encourage ran-

dom interactions, casual conversations, and accidental encounters.[14] "Chance favors the prepared mind," said Louis Pasteur.
Part of the preparation is building a network of relationships.

■

Success is social: It depends on our relationships with others. All
the ingredients of success that we customarily think of as "individual"—natural talent, intelligence, education, effort, and
luck—are intricately intertwined with networks. This reconsid-
eration of success demonstrates why it's useful to unlearn the
lessons of individual achievement, revising our perspective of
the world and how it operates. This change of perspective lib-
erates us from the myth of individualism and enables us to appreciate the power of social capital in achieving personal and
business success.

■ The Business Case for Social Capital

You might agree that many aspects of success are social in nature, but still be skeptical when it comes to the world of business. I'm frequently asked, "Where's the evidence that networks
improve business performance? And I mean *hard* evidence, not
just success stories and anecdotes!" This is a critical question; I
would ask it, too. After all, the message that networks play a key
role in personal and business success challenges conventional
wisdom. It calls for us to see the world in a different way, and to
change our behavior accordingly. It's no wonder we feel a sense
of danger. By changing our perspective and behaviors, whatever
worked in the past—the old winning formula, so to speak—it
may seem as if we'll lose our competitive edge.

This worry is natural, but it is unfounded. Learning to
move beyond individualism will increase success even in the
hard-nosed world of business.

The facts about social capital that I'm about to share with you are based on hard evidence—scientific findings from rigorous, quantitative research studies conducted by professional social scientists (sociologists, psychologists, economists, and political scientists). The concept of social capital has a long intellectual history; this practical book stands on a sturdy scholarly foundation.[15] Over the past twenty years or so, social scientists have documented the benefits of social capital for individuals and for organizations. Here is a sample of these benefits, starting with personal ones and then moving on to the benefits for the organization.

Getting a Job

Getting a job is one of the best-known uses of networks. The vast majority of people don't find jobs through advertisements, headhunters, electronic bulletin boards (like monster.com), or other "formal" methods. These methods work, of course, and you should never neglect them. But more people find jobs through personal contacts than by any other means. (The reverse is also true: most employers find good people by tapping networks of personal contacts. In fact, some companies institute organized programs to encourage workers to refer their contacts to the company.[16])

The practice of networking to find jobs has always been part of the conventional wisdom promoted by employment counselors and outplacement consultants. This conventional wisdom is supported by scientific research, beginning with Mark Granovetter's seminal study.[17] The hard evidence shows that most people find jobs through personal contacts; they find better paying, more satisfying jobs than the ones available through formal channels; and they stay at these jobs longer.

Pay and Promotions

People with rich social capital are paid better, promoted faster, and promoted at younger ages. This fact has been documented in many studies, here and abroad.[18] Sociologist Ron Burt of the

University of Chicago Graduate School of Business and INSEAD pioneered this line of research.[19] He discovered that social capital in the form of entrepreneurial opportunities yields these rewards. Entrepreneurial opportunities arise when a network contains many "structural holes" or gaps. A structural hole means a person is linked with two other people who are not themselves directly connected. The potential for creating value is obvious. Suppose, for example, that you have a tie with Bob in the Engineering Department (formed when you used to work with him) and a tie with Sue from Sales (formed when you both served on a company-wide task force). Bob and Sue don't know each other; in fact, they are unaware of each other's existence. You learn that Sue wants information about the needs of a new client. You know that Bob used to work there. By putting Bob and Sue together, you create value by bridging the structural hole. Sue will be grateful for your assistance; Bob will appreciate having a link with someone in Sales whom he can call on in the future. Both will be inclined to reciprocate at some point in the future, helping you by providing information, ideas, or contacts.

People are paid better, promoted faster, and promoted at younger ages when they create value. That is why social capital is related to these benefits: people create value out of their social capital. Problems seek solutions; solutions seek problems. If you bridge disparate parts of the organization, you can link a problem in one group with a solution from another. You will get more information, more quickly (you will have the luck-creating "spiderweb structure"). You can find financial, political, and social support for your projects.

Influence and Effectiveness

Influence stems from various sources—formal authority, coercion (control of punishments), expertise, and one's position in networks of workflow, communication, and friendship.[20] In today's organizations, formal authority and coercion are declining as important and effective sources of power, while expertise and network position are rising.[21] Becoming a "network builder" is a critical part of becoming a manager; seasoned managers who take charge of new situations are more likely to be successful if they attend to their network-building responsibilities, not just technical tasks.[22] Those who become central in an organization's networks are more influential and even paid better, compared with those who occupy peripheral network positions.[23] And managers who have an accurate mental map of the networks—who talks with whom, who's friends with whom, who gets along, who doesn't—are more influential and effective than peers who operate with an incomplete or distorted image of the networks.[24]

Venture Capital and Financing

Social capital doesn't stop with the individual benefits discussed in the last few sections—it is critical to the acquisition of venture capital. The U.S. Small Business Administration sponsored a series of surveys to examine how start-ups and new businesses get venture capital.[25] The findings are startling: Seventy-five percent of start-ups and new businesses find and secure financing through the "informal investing grapevine"—the social networks of capital seekers and investors. Capital seekers and providers find each other via friends, colleagues, acquaintances, and well-connected business associates such as attorneys, insurance agents, and accountants. This "informal capital market" is estimated to be so large that the amount of capital it provides is much greater than the financing supplied via the professional venture capital market.

Relationships also play a critical role in financing for "middle market" or midsized firms. Companies that develop personal relationships with their bankers get financing at lower rates, compared with companies that maintain arm's-length relationships.[26] You might be even more surprised to learn that social networks play a major role in decisions to purchase the stock of giant companies, too, such as those traded on the New York Stock Exchange. Polls of investors reveal that most institutional and individual investors decide to buy based on information from a friend or business associate, or because they know someone who bought the stock. Contrary to popular wisdom, few investors make decisions using such impersonal techniques as sophisticated technical analysis of a company's fundamentals.[27] My research shows that social networks influence the brokers and traders on the floors of the organized financial exchanges.[28]

Organizational Learning—and Doing

How does organizational learning take place? It's not by the use of formal knowledge management systems, argue Jeffery Pfeffer and Robert Sutton, because these systems "rarely reflect the fact that essential knowledge, including technical knowledge, is often transferred between people by stories, gossip, and by watching one another work."[29] As much as 70 percent of learning in the workplace takes place via informal interactions, according to a 1998 study by the Center for Workforce Development.[30] Smart companies master knowledge and put it into action by building social capital as an organizational competence. These organizational cultures promote—indeed, celebrate—learning by doing, teaching and coaching and mentoring, sharing good ideas and spreading best practices, and cooperating and collaborating rather than competing with others.[31]

Word-of-Mouth Marketing

Advertising increases awareness of products and services, but personal referrals and recommendations lead to actual decisions to purchase them.[32] Over four thousand empirical studies document the prominent role of social networks in the *diffusion* or spread of products and services as diverse as hybrid corn, luxury automobiles, best-selling books, men's and boys' undergarments, computer hardware and software, stocks and bonds, consulting services, computing services, and speaking engagements—to name just a few.[33] The word-of-mouth effect offers a virtual "free ride." So the best marketers incorporate systematic word-of-mouth programs in their marketing campaigns, tapping the power of social networks to launch new products and services, and to ensure the saturation of the market for existing ones.

Strategic Alliances

Social capital influences the use, performance, and success of strategic alliances. For example, compatible alliance partners often find each other via their social and business contacts. Prestigious firms in high-technology fields attract alliance partners; those who ally with these prestigious partners boost their own status and credibility, while the prestigious firms acquire access to new technologies.[34] Past alliances predict future alliances, too. Research shows that the more strategic alliances a company creates, the more it will create in the future.[35] Corning, for example, has evolved into what it calls a "network of alliances." It has mastered the art and business of strategic alliances, learning how to manage alliances and make them mutually beneficial. Companies like Corning make excellent partners, attracting even more alliance candidates.

Mergers and Acquisitions

Good social capital enables executives to successfully resist takeover attempts. Members of a top management team who are well connected in elite social and business circles—serving on other corporate boards and on nonprofit boards, having held high political offices, or serving as officers or trustees of trade associations—are better able to deter or fend off hostile takeover bids, compared with a top team of isolated executives.[36] A well-connected top management team is more likely to learn about and use effective takeover defenses. Indeed, new takeover defenses such as the poison pill diffuse through the network of interlocked corporate boards; central firms in the director interlock network learn about and adopt new defenses earlier than peripheral firms.[37] Bankruptcy is also less likely for firms with well-connected executives and board members, even controlling for a host of other explanations.[38]

Democracy

Doing business in other countries requires stable, honest, responsive, and dependable governments. The quality of government, however, varies with the richness of social capital—networks of cooperation, norms of civic engagement, and a spirit of trust. For example, as Harvard political scientist Robert Putnam found in his twenty-five-year study of democracy in Italy, the regions with rich social capital enjoy strong economic development and responsive local governments but the regions with poor social capital suffer.[39] Recently, Putnam traced a decline over time of the American propensity to join voluntary groups and associations, coining the phrase "bowling alone" (from the observed rise of solo versus team play in the game of ten pin bowling) to represent the downward trend in this form of social capital.[40] Other analyses dispute his claims of a decline of American social capital—but not his argument that democracy requires social capital. Without it, democracy withers or never takes root.[41]

■ Beyond the Business Case: Social Capital and the Quality of Life

As compelling as the business case for social capital is, there are even more compelling reasons to learn how to develop and use social capital. Rigorous studies published in psychology and medicine demonstrate a direct link between social capital and the quality, purpose, and meaning of life.

Happiness

When Sigmund Freud was asked for the secret of happiness, he replied: "Work and love." University of Chicago psychologist Mihaly Csikszentmihalyi has confirmed Freud's wisdom. Based on twenty-five years of psychological research on happiness, he finds that two factors matter more than anything else—meaningful work and the quality of relationships with others.[42] New "relational theories" of psychology argue that a primary motivation in life is *participation*: growth and development in connection with others.[43] Developing social networks leads to happiness, growth, satisfaction, and a meaningful life. Social networks, psychologist Barton Hirsch says, "involve far more than provision of narrow categories of 'help.' Instead, networks reflect the nature and value of our participation in the major life spheres."[44] The grand purpose of building social networks, then, is to enhance our participation in relationships with others and to make our contributions to the world. Happiness *must* ensue.

Health

People with good networks enjoy better mental and physical health. The health-enhancing effects of relationships have been documented in a host of studies, ranging from reduced risk of serious illnesses to freedom from the common cold.[45] (See the following case study for more on this.) Among people who become ill, those with solid support networks recover faster, compared with others who are isolated or alone.[46] Couples who treat each other with respect are less likely to suffer from infectious illnesses; conversely, unhappy marriages increase the risk of illness by 35 percent and shorten life expectancy by four years.[47]

Can Social Networks Prevent the Common Cold?

The answer is *yes,* according to a study reported in the *Journal of the American Medical Association.* "More diverse social networks were associated with greater resistance to upper respiratory illness," conclude researchers from Carnegie Mellon University.

How do they know? First, 276 healthy volunteers, age eighteen to fifty-five, were asked to describe their ties to friends, family, work, and community. Next, the researchers gave them nasal drops containing one of two rhinoviruses, the germs that cause the common cold. They placed the volunteers in quarantine, and waited to see who caught a cold. Those with more diverse social ties were much less likely to catch cold, compared with those with few types of social ties.

In the researchers' words: "In response to both viruses, those with more types of social ties were less susceptible to common colds, produced less mucus, were more effective in ciliary clearance of their nasal passages, and shed less virus. These relationships were unaltered by statistical controls for prechallenge virus-specific antibody, virus type, age, sex, season, body mass index, education, and race. Susceptibility to colds decreased in a dose-response manner with increased diversity of the social network. There was an adjusted relative risk of 4.2 comparing persons with fewest (1 to 3) to those with most (6 or more) types of social ties. Although smoking, poor sleep quality, alcohol abstinence, low dietary intake of vitamin C, elevated catecholamine levels, and being introverted were all associated with greater susceptibility to colds, they could only partially account for the relation between social network diversity and incidence of colds."

Source: S. Cohen, W. J. Doyle, D. P. Skoner, B. S. Rabin, and G. M. Gwaltney Jr., "Social Ties and Susceptibility to the Common Cold," *Journal of the American Medical Association* 277 (June 25, 1997):1940–1944.

Longer Life

Probably the most surprising finding is that people with good networks actually live longer.[48] All the mechanisms are not fully understood, but the link between networks and longevity appears to be caused by both behavioral and biological changes. For example, it has been widely observed that frequent attendance at religious services reduces mortality, partly due to behavioral changes—the tendency to make more social contacts, to improve health practices (stop smoking, reduce alcohol consumption), and to stay married—but also due to the meaning to life religion gives.[49] Lisa Berkman, M.D., now chair of the Department of Health and Social Behavior at the Harvard School of Public Health, mapped the social networks, lifestyles, and health behaviors of seven thousand residents of Alameda County, California, following them over nine years.[50] She discovered that isolated people were three times more likely to die during the nine years than the well-connected. The life-lengthening effect of connections was enjoyed regardless of age, notes Berkman's colleague Edward Hallowell, M.D., and significant effects persisted even in the presence of unhealthy practices such as smoking or obesity.[51] Her study and findings have been replicated more than a dozen times in the United States and around the world.[52] In addition to documenting the link between social networks and longer life, she learned that the specific *type* of connection didn't matter as much as having an assortment of connections. As Hallowell summarizes:

> To gain the benefits of connection, it didn't matter what kind of connection a person had. For example, you could live alone, but have frequent contact with friends or relatives, and be protected. Or you could belong to various voluntary organizations, but not participate in any religious activity, and still be protected. Or your connection could come from church and family, but not from any volunteer organization, and you would still be protected. The key to gaining the benefits of connection was to have several kinds of connection, but the kinds could vary from person to person.[53]

■

This brief tour of the business case for social capital—and the case beyond the business case—provides ample evidence of the benefits of building personal and business networks. Better networks improve wealth, health, and happiness. Individuals *and* organizations reap the benefits of better networks. That's good news. The even better news is that all of us can learn how to build better networks. In my experience, anyone can improve networks. This book shows the way. But there's a catch. If we create networks with the sole intention of *getting something,* we won't succeed. We can't *pursue* the benefits of networks; the benefits *ensue* from investments in meaningful activities and relationships. This is a radical reorientation to the "use" of networks, and so I don't expect everyone to accept it without hesitation. This reorientation stands on an ethical argument about the proper use of social capital. I introduce the argument next, and will pick it up again and elaborate it in subsequent chapters.

■ The Ethics of Using Social Capital

Many people incorrectly interpret the message of social capital as blatant manipulation: building and using relationships for self-serving and instrumental goals, even for nefarious purposes. Over the years I've given many talks and seminars about networks and social capital to a wide variety of audiences. One of the most frequent concerns I've heard is the ethics of managing relationships. Consider Vivian, a departmental manager who attended one of my seminars on building social capital. After reviewing the results of my diagnosis of personal and business networks (the subject of Chapter Two), she and I discussed why and how one might want to change a network. Vivian had learned through her diagnosis that her core network was small and the people in it were very similar. She felt it didn't support her mission and goals. So we discussed the possibility of including more people in her core network. We also discussed the possibility of ending certain relationships with others. Vivian couldn't contain herself. "I don't want to *think* about adding or dropping people from my network! It's unethical to think about people as things you can add and drop!"

Vivian's declaration, as you can imagine, ignited our discussion. Is it somehow unethical to consciously "manage" a network? The fact is that you can't *avoid* deliberate decisions about your networks of relationships. It turned out that Vivian often made decisions to add or drop people from her networks. She had been married, divorced, and remarried (decisions to add, drop, and add to her networks). She and her first husband had gone through intensive marriage counseling. Even though they eventually divorced, the choice of counseling indicates a conscious decision to attempt to repair the relationship. With her second husband, Vivian consciously decided to have two children (decisions to add people). She and her husband are loving, attentive, devoted parents who began a college fund for each child soon after each one was born (decisions to invest in relationships). At work, Vivian made regular personnel decisions, hiring, retaining, and firing people in her department (decisions to add, keep, and drop members of her networks and the networks of everyone in her department). And, of course, Vivian *did* think carefully about all of these decisions to add and drop people from her networks.

It would have been unethical for Vivian to *not* think about decisions as important as marriage, divorce, children, hiring, and firing. I argue that the same is true for any relationship, from the strongest, deepest connections we have to the most transitory, fleeting interactions with strangers. All of these can be life-giving, life-enhancing, meaningful contacts with another human being—what Hallowell calls "human moments."[54] The word for "hello" in some aboriginal tongues means "I see you"—a statement of acknowledgment and recognition. In contrast, I've walked through a factory with a plant manager who never even nodded to the workers and supervisors he supposedly managed. And I've seen companies downsize with an utter disregard for the effects on relationships, internal and external, devastating the social networks that knit the company together.[55] All behaviors and decisions about relationships have ethical implications, whether or not we consciously consider the ethics of our actions and decisions.

We manage even our best and most fulfilling relationships. After all, good relationships don't just happen. Humans are imperfect beings living in an imperfect world. Conflict is inevitable in any relationship, given that each person in a relationship has a different background, lifestyle, interests, values, and needs. The critical issue is how we manage the conflict. Is that the same as manipulation?

It is possible, of course, to cultivate a false trust relationship for the purpose of deceit and abuse. The world is full of people who engage in such practices, ranging from the unethical salesperson who uses social psychological principles of influence to induce sales to the professional swindler who uses the same principles to defraud victims, as my colleague Rob Faulkner and I learned in our investigation of a business that bilked hundreds of investors out of millions of dollars.[56] But any body of knowledge can be used for moral or immoral purposes. It's not the management of relationships—or social psychology itself—that is unethical. It's what we do with our knowledge that makes our practices ethical or not.

Each of us makes decisions all the time about our relationships, consciously or not, that have ethical implications. Suppose, for example, that you find yourself in the situation I described earlier: you discover the "structural hole" between

Sue and Bob. What do you do with it? The ethical decision is to bring Sue and Bob together. Another possibility, however, would be to keep them apart and exploit the structural hole. You could, for example, secretly interrogate Bob about his former client, pumping him for information that might be useful to Sue. Then you could bring what you learned to Sue, representing it as your own, and never revealing your "sources." Sue, of course, would be grateful for the information. Bob would be indifferent, though he might wonder about your sudden curiosity about his former employer. You have profited, but you did so by concealment. And you lost a golden opportunity to help others by helping them to build relationships. Ethics aside, this sort of behavior can be profitable, but in the long run it is inherently self-limiting, even self-defeating.

"If you want to go north, head south." This old Zen saying is true for social capital. If we try to build social capital directly we won't succeed. Viktor Frankl, the Austrian psychologist who developed logotherapy based partly on his experiences in a Nazi death camp (which he wrote about in *Man's Search for Meaning*) addresses the paradox of happiness.[57] Anyone who tries to pursue happiness directly will fail and be unhappy. Happiness cannot be *pur*sued; it *en*sues from the pursuit of worthwhile, meaningful activities. If a person joins an association just to "network," people see right through the false front. But if you join an association you believe in—one that has a mission you are passionate about—you will form new relationships as a natural by-product of your involvement with the association. Social capital is the by-product, sometimes a very deliberate and conscious by-product, of the pursuit of meaningful activities.

I am acquainted with a bank loan officer in Chicago, Janet, whose behavior is the epitome of what I call "the paradox of taking yourself out of the equation." Janet was successful, but she wanted to be extraordinarily successful. Her job was to make loans, and she was evaluated on the volume of loans she produced. One day she experienced a shift of perspective. She stopped trying to make loans and started trying to help. Instead of looking at the person across from her desk as a loan to be made, Janet saw the person as someone with needs that she might be able to help satisfy. If she thought they didn't need a loan, she would tell them so, even if they qualified for one according to her bank's rules. If she thought her potential customers could do better by getting a loan at a competitor's bank, she would give them the name of a loan officer at the bank. Eventually, she engaged potential customers in a broad conversation about their lives, families, and needs, and then worked hard to help them, no matter what kind of help they needed. She even began the practice of sharing cab rides with strangers, just so she could strike up a conversation and see if there was some way she could assist them. What happened? All she helped were so grateful that they did everything they could to help her. Even if they didn't get a loan at her bank, they would recommend Janet to all of their friends, family, neighbors, business associates, colleagues, and just about anyone else. The result was an explosion in Janet's loan productivity. She made more loans—and made more money—than ever before. She had become *extraordinarily* successful by taking herself out of the equation and helping others without regard to how it might help her.

The ethics of social capital requires that we all recognize our moral duty to consciously manage relationships. No one can evade this duty—*not* managing relationships *is* managing them. The only choice is how to manage networks of relationships. To be an effective networker, we can't directly pursue the benefits of networks, or focus on what we can get from our networks. The best prescription is to take themselves out of the equation, focusing on how we can contribute to others. In practice, "using" social capital means putting our networks into action and service for others. The great paradox is that by contributing to others, you are helped in return, often far in excess of what anyone would expect or predict.

■ Shifting to the Network Paradigm

Both the business case for social capital and the case beyond the business case are nested in the nature of these changing times—a paradigm shift from a group to a network organization of life. Sociologists Barry Wellman and Keith Hampton call this a paradigm shift "from living in 'little boxes' to living in networked societies." As they describe it,

> Members of little-box societies deal only with fellow members of the few groups to which they belong: at home, in the neighborhood, at work, or in voluntary organizations. They belong to a discrete work group in a single organization; they live in a household in a neighborhood; they belong to a kinship group (one each for themselves and their spouse) and to discrete voluntary organizations. . . . All of these appear to be bodies with precise boundaries for inclusion (and therefore exclusion). . . . In such a society, each interaction remains in its place: one group at a time.
>
> Although people often view the world in groups . . . they function in networks. In networked societies boundaries are more permeable, interactions occur with diverse others, linkages switch between multiple networks, and hierarchies (when they exist) are flatter and more recursive.[58]

This book is an invitation to engage and participate in the shift to the network paradigm. It offers the concept of networks as a mental model, a lens, a mode of behavior, and a method of contribution. As a mental model, it is a way of thinking about the world and how it operates; as a lens, it is a way of viewing the world; as a mode of behavior, it is a way of acting in the world; and, as a method of contribution, it offers a way of making the world a better place by building networks, connecting the unconnected, and linking the unlinked.

CHAPTER SUMMARY

Social capital refers to the many resources available to us in and through our personal and business networks. These resources include information, ideas, leads, business opportunities, financial capital, power, emotional support, goodwill, trust, and cooperation. Without well-built and well-managed networks, however, these resources remain hidden. They also remain hidden if we take refuge in the myth of individualism, pretending that we are masters of our own fates, or that relationships really don't matter. Even natural talent, intelligence, education, effort, and luck are not individual attributes at all; they are developed, shaped, and expressed by and through relationships with others.

There is also a business case for social capital—hard evidence that social capital boosts business performance. Individuals who build and use social capital get better jobs, better pay, faster promotions, and are more influential and effective, compared with peers who are unable or unwilling to tap the power of social capital. Organizations with rich social capital enjoy access to venture capital and financing, improved organizational learning, the power of word-of-mouth marketing, the ability to create strategic alliances, and the resources to defend against hostile takeovers. And social capital is a bulwark of democracy.

The case beyond the business case links networks with the quality of life. A network of good relationships leads to happiness, satisfaction, and a meaningful life. A good network improves health and lengthens life. But it's more than that. Building networks is a major mode of participation and involvement in the world. Building networks enables each of us to contribute to others. Accordingly, there is a moral duty to consciously manage relationships, and to do so in ways that serve others. By doing so, we not only reap the personal benefits of networks, we make the world a better place by making it a more connected place.

Evaluating Your Social Capital

t's easy to get lost driving the back roads of New England. When lost visitors stop an old-timer for directions, he'll rub his jaw, peer into the distance, and drawl, "Well . . . you can't get there from here." This Yankee favorite contains a lesson for us: We can't get where we want to go (achieve our goals) unless we know where we are now (our social capital today). Your next step, therefore, is evaluation: using proven techniques to gain insights into the state and quality of your social capital. Evaluation gives you the "here." In Chapter Three, we'll address the "there"—your destination—and how you get there by building the right networks. And we'll foil our Yankee old-timer, proving that you *can* get there from here.

■ The Need to Evaluate Social Capital

Evaluating your social capital takes an investment of time, attention, and energy. You might be tempted to ask, Is it really necessary? Don't I already have a good enough idea of the size, structure, and composition of my networks to go right to learning how to use them? Surprisingly, most people don't have a very accurate picture of their networks. To see what I mean, consider this question and indicate your answer after it.

> Some people have friends who know one another. Other people have friends who don't know one another. Would you say that all of your friends know one another, most of your friends know one another, only a few of your friends know one another, or none of your friends know one another?

Check one box:
- ❏ All of my friends know one another
- ❏ Most of my friends know one another
- ❏ Only a few of my friends know one another
- ❏ None of my friends know one another

This question was asked in the General Social Survey (GSS), a scientific poll of the American population, based on a national probability sample.[1] It attempts to measure an important feature of personal networks—the extent to which one's close contacts are connected to each other—because "connections among connections" are a revealing indicator of social capital. Because it is so revealing, the reliability of this measure is critical: Does a person's *casual perception* of "connections among connections" match reality? For example, if a person perceives that "only a few of my friends know one another," is it factually true? Are most of the person's friends really strangers?

The answer might startle you: Most people's casual perceptions don't reflect reality. When answers to this GSS question are compared with data collected via rigorous sociometric methods (a set of techniques explored later in this chapter), it turns out that impressions of the extent to which friends know one another are virtually unrelated to the extent they did know one another. This inaccuracy in perceptions doesn't vary much by age, education, income, race, size of town, or marital status.[2]

Skeptical? Here's another question. Think of your spouse (if you are married) or a close peer (if you are not). Suppose I give you a list of twenty new products and services, such as an electric-powered automobile ("250 miles without a recharge"), a "hands-free" telephone ("talk and listen up to twenty feet"), a disposable "fashion" raincoat, a color TV that projects a picture on a large screen, and "investment counseling via closed circuit TV."[3] Could you accurately predict your spouse's or peer's preferences for each one? That is, could you rank these products and services according to this person's likes and dislikes? If you did this experiment, you would then ask your spouse or peer to tell you about his or her preferences, and you would compare that list against the one you prepared yourself, calculating your "predictive accuracy"—how well your list of predictions matches your spouse's or peer's stated preferences. How accurate do you think you would be? Indicate your estimate of "predictive accuracy" here:

Check one box:
- ❏ I would be very accurate (75 percent or higher predictive accuracy)
- ❏ I would be somewhat accurate (50–74 percent predictive accuracy)
- ❏ I would be somewhat inaccurate (25–49 percent predictive accuracy)
- ❏ I would be very inaccurate (less than 25 percent predictive accuracy)

Now consider a different task. Suppose you were given a list of twenty-one attitude statements, such as "I would like to spend a year in London or Paris," "I am an impulse buyer," "Television is my primary form of entertainment," and "I like to pay cash for everything I buy."[4] Taking the perspective of your spouse or peer, to what extent would she or he agree or disagree with each statement? As before, if you did this experiment, you would ask your spouse or peer to agree or disagree with each statement. You would than compare that list against the one you prepared, calculating your "predictive accuracy." How accurate would you be this time? Indicate your estimate here:

Check one box:
❑ I would be very accurate (75 percent or higher predictive accuracy)
❑ I would be somewhat accurate (50–74 percent predictive accuracy)
❑ I would be somewhat inaccurate (25–49 percent predictive accuracy)
❑ I would be very inaccurate (less than 25 percent predictive accuracy)

Colleagues at the University of Chicago Graduate School of Business ran these experiments with hundreds of subjects. Almost all of the participants were highly confident that they could accurately predict the preferences of spouses or peers. Most anticipated they would be 75 percent accurate or higher. Most weren't. For the twenty new products and services, the average predictive accuracy for spouses was only 7 percent! The accuracy of wives' predictions was not statistically different from the accuracy of husbands' predictions.[5] For the twenty-one attitude statements, the average predictive accuracy for spouses was 26 percent, and for peers, 28 percent.[6]

In short, most people *think* they understand the likes and dislikes of spouses and peers, but they don't. And if you really don't understand the preferences of people you are close to, what does that imply about mutual understanding in all the various types of relationships in your life?

The problem of inaccuracy is compounded because most people *think* their "mental maps" of the networks around them are accurate. For some, this problem gets worse when they discover their mental maps are inaccurate. They get *angry*. They don't like the challenge to their worldview and so flat-out reject the idea of understanding social capital. As you work through this chapter, you may discover that your casual image of your networks is inaccurate. If so, I invite you to place your discomfort aside and stay open to the ideas. Use the demonstration of inaccuracy as a motivator to update and improve your mental map.

A few lucky people do have mental maps that reliably represent the social terrain. Such people are much more effective and influential as a result.[7] You might be one of the lucky few. However, most people operate with inaccurate and incomplete mental maps, and many underestimate the value of social capital. As a result, they repeatedly commit any number of network blunders: They don't see or tap the resources available through their networks, and are thus much less successful than they could be; they hire (or fire) only on the basis of a person's human capital, not the strength of a person's social capital; they downsize without regard to the networks of formal and informal ties in an organization, ripping apart the social fabric of a company; they put people with inadequate social capital on a team and then wonder why the team doesn't perform well. I could go on but you get the point: Making decisions without an accurate mental map is like driving blindfolded through crowded city streets. The good news is that anyone can learn how to be a better observer and analyzer of networks.

■ Becoming a Better Observer

How do you know that a relationship exists between two people? Individuals are the only visible "units of observation." You can't see a relationship directly; it must be inferred from behaviors and cues. Yet appearances, as everyone knows, can be deceiving; any number of great comedies and tragedies are built on this premise. Consider this story of mistaken relationships in the world of high finance:

> At the height of his wealth and success, the financier Baron
> de Rothschild was petitioned for a loan by an acquaintance.
> Reputedly, the great man replied, "I won't give you a loan
> myself; but I will walk arm-in-arm with you across the floor
> of the Stock Exchange, and you soon shall have willing lenders
> to spare.[8]

Suppose you had been one of those who saw the great baron walking arm in arm with his acquaintance? Would you have been one of the willing lenders who assumed a close business relationship between the two men? Or would you have collected additional evidence to test your inference about the apparent relationship?

If you see two people together—walking down the street, leaving the office together, talking at a party—you probably make inferences about their relationship. I do the same. It's human nature. Most people maintain a continuous, automatic mental conversation about the people they observe and the relationships they infer among them. Good observers of networks, however, put this internal conversation on hold. They recognize the natural tendency to make incorrect inferences. They know that inaccuracy runs both ways, inferring relationships when none exist (the case of the baron and his acquaintance), or assuming that relationships don't exist when they do. So good observers start from the position that they *don't know* rather than that they do know. They acknowledge that they are probably wrong rather than probably right.

Astute observers of networks develop working hypotheses about people and their relationships, seeking additional evidence to confirm, modify, or disconfirm their first impressions. Consider a practice Charles Darwin (*The Origin of Species*) developed during his five-year voyage as a naturalist aboard *HMS Beagle*. Most people would probably be quick to make a record of observations that supported a pet idea. Darwin, however, made a special effort to jot down *disconfirming* evidence, knowing that the mind naturally tends to forget facts that don't fit one's pet theory. Anyone can become a better observer by doing the same. The scientific techniques reviewed next can help you to evaluate your networks more accurately and systematically.

■ Using Sociometric Techniques to Observe Networks

Observation is a skill. There are entire books about the subject that help to hone it (John Lofland's classic *Analyzing Social Settings* comes to mind).[9] Here, I present a set of techniques developed in the academic specialty called "social network analysis."[10] The field's roots go back to the 1930s, when psychiatrist Jacob Moreno invented "psychological geography," an analytical and visual display of the network of relationships in a group or community. The publication of Moreno's invention made such a splash that it was described in the *New York Times* under the title "Emotions Mapped by New Geography."[11] The story was carried by newspapers across the nation. Later, Moreno and others introduced sociometry, the scientific measurement of social networks. Today, network analysis is a vast and active field of research, attracting scholars from sociology, communications, anthropology, social psychology, applied mathematics, and statistics. Analysts study networks in a diversity of settings, including groups, organizations, industries, and markets. They have even analyzed brain structures and criminal networks.[12] The field has produced increasingly sophisticated and powerful methods for measuring and analyzing networks. Some are so powerful that network analysts have voiced worries that the techniques could be misused and abused.[13] Suppose, for example, that an unscrupulous plant manager wants to sabotage a mounting unionization effort. The manager could collect and analyze network data on the workforce, search for friendship cliques containing known informal leaders, and then fire all members of the cliques. Fortunately, abuses are rare; most network analyses of organizations are used to identify and fix organizational design problems such as communication bottlenecks or workflow inefficiencies. The sole intention of the sociometric techniques described here is to provide you with insights into your networks so that you can build social capital and use it constructively, remembering that manipulative and hypocritical uses of social capital tend to be self-defeating.

In this discussion I focus on sociometric techniques that reveal the basic patterns of personal and business networks. Sociologists and others have refined and advanced these techniques over the years. For example, the pioneers of the field devised ingenious survey methods that measure *egocentric* networks.[14] An egocentric network is the set of relationships centered around a person, or *ego*. Those who have direct links with ego are called *alters*. The Topical Module on Social Networks in the General Social Survey (GSS) fielded by the National Opinion Research Center demonstrated that egocentric networks could be measured via a national survey. (You will see some of the results shortly.) Sociologist Ron Burt pioneered the use of sociometric techniques to study social capital in business organizations.[15] Many others have contributed to this stream of work, exploring and perfecting ways to evaluate social capital in the world of business.[16] The techniques presented in this chapter are grounded in this long line of research and have been developed further through my applied research with HUMAX Corporation, an assessment and training firm specializing in personal and organizational development. (For information on Web-administered tools for evaluating social capital, you can visit the HUMAX Web site at http://www.HUMAXnetworks.com.)

The first step is to describe your networks by means of a sociometric survey. Your answers to the survey questions will supply the raw materials that you will use to diagnose your social capital. Consider each question thoughtfully; the better data you provide, the better the diagnosis of your social capital. If you aren't sure of an answer, conduct an additional test of your working hypothesis and then return to answer the question.

The survey will take some time for you to complete. If you take it seriously, and take your time, you can gain some deep insights into your social capital. Consider it an investment, one that will pay off again and again in the future.

After you complete the survey, you then start the process of diagnosing your networks. This involves the calculation of a few basic network measures. A number of worksheets are provided to assist you. Finally, you'll see how to interpret the information, drawing conclusions about your social capital.

■ Sociometric Survey

You begin with a few questions about your personal and business networks. These questions are memory probes that illuminate certain areas and features of your core network. Of course, you know many more people than you can name in any sociometric survey. Research shows, however, that it isn't necessary to enumerate your total network. A *sample* of your total network, collected via a sociometric instrument, represents the main patterns and tendencies of your network, suggesting the essential nature of your social capital.

A Few Questions About Your Networks

Before you continue, take a few moments to think about the people you know from different areas of your life, such as work, family, community, and so on. To jog your memory, you may want to consult your Rolodex file, business cards, holiday lists, e-mail address book, Palm Pilot, and so on. You will draw upon this information in completing the survey.

How you answer each question in Worksheet 2.1 is entirely up to you. Think broadly; you can name anyone you want, from any part of your life. Each question specifies a maximum number of responses, but you don't have to fill in all the blanks if you don't feel it's accurate. You can repeat names across questions, but you don't have to. (Note: Throughout this chapter, you may want to reproduce the worksheets on separate sheets of paper or enlarge them on a photocopy machine.) When you're ready, complete Worksheet 2.1.

Some Questions About the People You Named

Now, review your answers to the four questions in Worksheet 2.1. In the first column of Worksheet 2.2, write the names of the people you identified in Worksheet 2.1. Don't repeat names on the worksheet; if you named someone more than once, write down the person's name only once. The maximum number of names you could have on Worksheet 2.2 is twenty. This would occur if you filled in every blank for the four questions in Worksheet 2.1 *and* you never repeated a name. This seldom occurs, however, so don't worry if you have fewer than twenty names.

After you have completed listing the people you named, answer the additional questions on Worksheet 2.2. Be sure you

■ Worksheet 2.1. Questions About Your Networks ■

Question 1. From time to time most people discuss important matters with other people. Looking back over the last six months, who are the people with whom you discussed matters important to you? (List as few or as many names as you want, up to a maximum of 5 names.)

_____

_____

_____

_____

_____

Question 2. Consider the people you communicate with in order to get your work done. (Your *work* is your principal occupation or main activity.) Of all the people you have communicated with during the last six months, who has been the most important for getting your work done? (List as few or as many names as you want, up to a maximum of 5 names.)

_____

_____

_____

_____

_____

Question 3. Now, consider an important new project or initiative that you are promoting. Consider the people who would be influential for getting it approved or obtaining resources you need. Who would you talk with to get support for your project? (List as few or as many names as you want, up to a maximum of 5 names.)

_____

_____

_____

_____

_____

Question 4. Who do you socialize with? *Socializing* includes spending time with people after working hours, visiting one another at home, going to social events, going out for meals, and so on. Over the last six months, who are the main people with whom you have socialized informally? (List as few or as many names as you want, up to a maximum of 5 names.)

_____

_____

_____

_____

_____

■ Worksheet 2.2. Describing the People in Your Networks ■

Name	Male or Female?	Highest level of formal education?	Age?	Race or ethnicity?	What is this person's main relationship to you: work, family, or other?	Significant experience living or working abroad?
1.						
2.						
3.						
4.						
5.						
6.						
7.						
8.						
9.						
10.						
11.						
12.						
13.						
14.						
15.						
16.						
17.						
18.						
19.						
20.						

answer each question for each person you named. These additional questions cover basic demographic characteristics, such as age and education. If you're not sure about an answer, you can estimate—or, even better, conduct an additional test! (Ask the person.)

Questions About Your Affiliations

Next, let's consider your active involvement with various types of associations, groups, and organizations. By *types*, I mean categories of associations, groups, or organizations. Consider, for example, the first type listed in Worksheet 2.3, "professional association." This is considered one category, even though a person could be involved with two or more professional associations. CEO Tom Caprel, for example, whom you will meet later in this chapter, is an active member of two professional associations, but these two count for only one type. The point of counting types is to capture the *diversity* of external ties, rather than the sheer number of them.

By *active involvement*, I mean regular attendance at events and meetings held by a group, face-to-face interactions with people associated with it, and, in general, participation in the group's life. The point here is to capture your engagement in a group's networks. Accordingly, membership and active involvement are not the same. For example, you could be a formal member "on paper" but not be actively involved in a group's life; or, conversely, you could be actively involved with a group but never become a formal member. If you are somehow affiliated with a group but not engaged in its networks, then you are not actively involved according to this definition. So, for example, you might be on the membership rolls of a political party so you can vote in its primaries, donate money to the party, and vote for its candidates on election day, but you are not actively involved with the political party unless you attend the party's

■ Worksheet 2.3. Describing Your Affiliations ■	
Type of Affiliation	Actively Involved?
Professional association	
Trade or industry association	
Political party	
Church or religious organization	
Charitable or philanthropic organization	
Sports club or recreation organization	
Art, music, or cultural organization	
Alumni or school related group	
Self-help or personal development group	
Other (not named above)	
TOTAL (add number of checkmarks in column)	

meetings, do volunteer work that brings you into contact with others, and the like. Similarly, you might be a lifelong believer in a certain religion but you are not actively involved unless you also participate regularly in events, services, or social activities sponsored by a religious group or organization.

Consider each type in Worksheet 2.3, and indicate your involvement with each one during the last six months. If you are not affiliated with a particular type, don't check its box. Just leave the row blank for that type.

Diagnosing Your Networks

Answering this sociometric survey has generated a sample that suggests the patterns and tendencies in your larger networks. Your next task is to assemble these raw materials in a way that helps you see these patterns and tendencies. The upcoming sections address the assembly process in steps, pausing now and then to discuss the implications for social capital. You'll begin by depicting your networks graphically. Then you'll analyze them in terms of three dimensions: size, composition, and focus. You'll pull everything together in the final section of the chapter, ending with some conclusions about the nature of your social capital.

■ Picturing Your Networks

A picture's worth a thousand words. Visualizing your networks reveals some basic features about the nature of your social capital. The next step, therefore, is to draw a sociogram for each of the four networks represented by the questions in Worksheet 2.1. The examples in Figure 2.1 will give you an idea of what to do. Get a pad of paper, or pull a blank sheet from your printer. Review your answers to the questions in Worksheet 2.1, one question at a time, and follow these instructions for each question in turn:

Write your name at the center, and arrange the names from your list around you.

Consider the relationship you have with each person. Draw a line between you and the person to represent the link.

Consider the links among the people you named, that is, the "connections among your connections." Draw a line between two people if they know each other personally; don't draw a line if the two people are strangers or aren't really acquainted with each other.

What can you learn from picturing your networks? The four sociograms you just drew provide the first clues to your

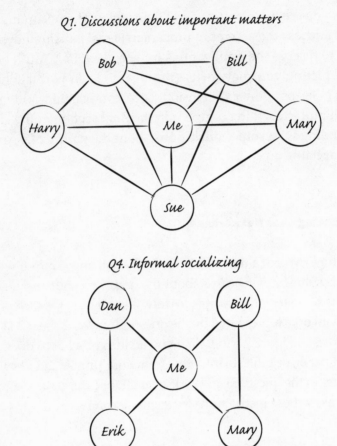

Figure 2.1. Picturing Your Networks: Two Examples of Sociograms

social capital. Consider Bill's and Sue's sociograms in Figure 2.2. As you can see, their egocentric networks are similar. Each network contains the same *number* of people: Sue is directly connected to six people and Bill is directly connected to six people. Sue and Bill are members of the same "group" (labeled Group 1 in Figure 2.2). The big difference, of course, is the pattern of "connections among connections." These are represented by solid lines in Figure 2.2. All of Bill's direct ties are within Group 1. Sue

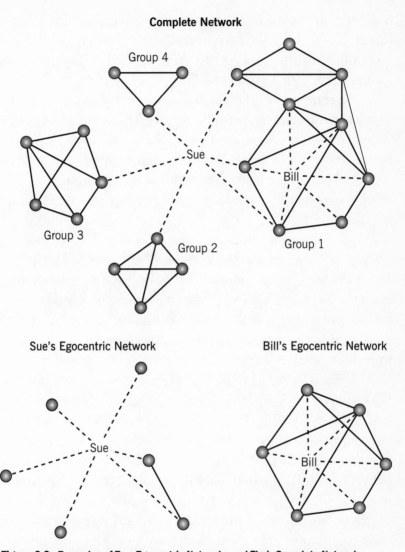

Figure 2.2. **Examples of Two Egocentric Networks and Their Complete Network**
Source: Inspired by network diagrams in Ronald S. Burt, "The Network Structure of Social Capital," in Robert I. Sutton and Barry M. Staw (eds.), *Research in Organizational Behavior* (Greenwich, Conn.: JAI Press, 2000).

has ties to members of Group 1, but she also has ties that extend out of the Group. As shown in the "complete network," these ties make her the "bridge" to three otherwise unconnected groups (Groups 2, 3, and 4).

The comparison of these two egocentric networks with the larger network they represent illustrates a basic principle of networks: The more connections among connections you have, the more likely your larger network is closed, folding back in on itself. Conversely, the fewer connections among connections you have, the more likely your larger network is open, extending out into the world.

Bill's sociogram illustrates what is called a "closed" or "clique" network. Sue's is an example of an "open" or what Ron Burt calls an "entrepreneurial" network.[17] What's so entrepreneurial about Sue's network? As Burt has shown, managers with this structure are likely to get information and to get it first, and they are likely to discover opportunities as they emerge.[18] Sue is more likely than Bill to get news as it breaks no matter where it breaks. She is therefore more likely to spot new opportunities as they emerge. Suppose that Group 2 in Figure 2.2 represents the key engineers in the Manufacturing Design Department, and Group 3 represents the leaders of the Sales Department. Given her position as a bridge between the two, Sue could act as a go-between, negotiating between the two often-conflicting departments. Or, she might learn of a customer problem identified by the sales staff (Group 3), and bring it to the attention of the design engineers (Group 2). In this case, Sue creates value by bringing together two otherwise disconnected people or groups.

Don't draw the conclusion that an entrepreneurial network like Sue's is always better than a closed network like Bill's. It depends, for example, on the context of the network. Suppose the complete network in Figure 2.2 represents a small company (Group 1) and its three main clients (Groups 2–4). Sue is the relationship manager for these clients, each of whom puts unreasonable demands on Sue and her company. These cross-pressures can be a source of stress and strain for Sue.[19] Bill could be the informal leader of the small company (Group 1). His closed network would enable him to coordinate the efforts of its members and to maintain the company's internal cohesiveness. Nonetheless, the main conclusion from various studies is that entrepreneurial networks yield higher performance, compared with closed networks. Networks like Sue's are more apt than those like Bill's are to lead to the business benefits discussed in Chapter One, such as getting a job, better pay, faster promotions, and greater influence and effectiveness.[20]

Just eyeballing a sociogram can give you an idea of how open or closed it is. For example, it's obvious that Sue's sociogram is much more open than Bill's. Examine your four sociograms. Do they look more like Sue's open network, or more like Bill's closed network? The differences between networks are not always that obvious, so you need to be more precise, and use a few basic network measures to aid your diagnosis.

Size

The diagnostic process began by focusing on the extent to which networks are open or closed, as shown by the configuration of connections among connections. That's because the *structure* of a network matters more than its *size*. To put it another way, the arrangement of ties is more important than the number of ties. This is a fundamental tenet of network theory, and it is one of the best-documented findings in network research. For example, Sue's and Bill's sociograms in Figure 2.2 show that they both have the same number of ties, but the connections among connections are utterly different. Sue is the bridge between lots of otherwise unconnected people; Bill, in contrast, tends to have connections with people who are connected with each other.

A simple measure called *density* helps to indicate the extent of connections among connections. Density is the number of actual relationships among alters in a network, expressed as a percentage of the maximum number of relationships possible given the number of alters in the network.[21] Density varies between 0 percent and 100 percent. If all of the alters in a network are connected to each other, then density equals 100 percent. This is a closed network. If all of the alters are completely disconnected from each other, then density equals 0 percent. This is an open network. For example, there is only one connection among the six alters in Sue's network (represented by the single solid line). The maximum number of connections among connections possible in a network with six alters is fifteen. So the density of her network is 1 divided by 15, or about 7 percent. There are eight connections among the six alters in Bill's network (represented by the nine solid lines). The density of his network is 9 divided by 15, or about 60 percent. The density of Bill's network indicates that it is closed, compared with Sue's, but it could be even more closed. He would need to have six more connections among his alters to reach 100 percent density.

A high density of connections among alters signals that a network contains *redundancy*.[22] For example, your relationships with two alters are redundant when the alters are connected directly to each other. This redundancy doesn't mean that the two alters are replaceable or interchangeable. Rather, it implies something important about what I call "networking reach." Every alter has his or her own egocentric network, just as you do. An alter's egocentric network is a gateway into the larger world of networks. Your direct link with an alter can grant you access to the alter's egocentric network; it may also give you access to a chain of links—an alter's alter's network, an alter's alter's alter's network, and so on. But if your alters are redundant, their networks tend to coincide; they are connected to the same set of people. If their networks coincide, your networking reach into the larger world of networks is constrained. In contrast, if your alters are not interconnected, their egocentric networks don't tend to overlap, and your networking reach is wider and broader, extending farther into the world.

To illustrate, look back at Bill's and Sue's networks in Figure 2.2. Bill's contains more redundancy than Sue's. His alters' egocentric networks tend to coincide, constraining his networking reach. Bill has, for example, few independent sources of information, due to the closed structure of his network. Sue's alters' networks tend to be separate; her network has almost no redundancy in it. So, for example, she enjoys the benefits of independent information sources.

Another way of thinking about redundancy is to contrast absolute size with "effective size."[23] Absolute size is just a count of the number of alters in a network. The absolute sizes of Sue's and Bill's networks are the same—six alters each. But the *effective* size of Bill's is much smaller, due to the redundancy in it. The more redundancy there is in a network, the more you have to "deflate" the absolute size of a network to determine its effective size.

There's one more way to think of the size and structure of your networks. Go back to the list of names you compiled in Worksheet 2.2. How many unique names did you come up with? If you filled in all the blanks for each question, and never repeated a name, you would have a maximum of twenty unique names. If you have fewer than twenty, then you didn't fill in all the blanks, or you repeated some names, or both. Most people who respond to a sociometric survey repeat some names. Repetition denotes that you have relationships with some of the same people for multiple reasons. For example, you may socialize informally with the same people you talk with about important matters. I use the term "overlap" to refer to this phenomenon, because repeating names means that different types of networks overlap each other.

Looking back at your list in Worksheet 2.2 and your four sociograms, how much overlap is there? That is, do you see the same or different names across the four sociograms? Are you the bridge between different worlds, so to speak, or do all your worlds coincide?

Consider each of your four sociograms and calculate the measures of absolute size, density, redundancy, and effective size for each one, using Worksheet 2.4 as a guide. (Note: these measures are undefined for a network with only one alter, or none at all. If you encounter this situation for one of your sociograms, skip the calculations for this sociogram and go to the next one.)

How big is each of your four egocentric networks? I can offer some comparative statistics for Question 1 in Worksheet 2.1, because this was asked in the General Social Survey (GSS) of the American population. And almost all researchers who measure egocentric networks begin with this GSS question. It is considered the best general-purpose question for sampling networks.[24] The bar chart in Figure 2.3 displays the distribution of responses. For me, the biggest surprise is that 7 percent of Americans say that they don't talk with *anyone* about important matters! An additional 15 percent say they talk about important matters with only *one* person. Putting these two together, you see that one in five Americans (22 percent) have tiny egocentric networks. The mode and the mean both are about three alters.[25] (For a cross-cultural comparison, the average is 3.3 in Tianjin, China's third-largest city.[26])

How dense is each egocentric network? Again, I can offer comparative statistics for Question 1 in Worksheet 2.1. The average density is 61 percent, meaning that over half of the maximum number of relationships possible among alters actually exists.[27]

■ Worksheet 2.4. Calculating the Density and Effective Size of Your Networks ■

NETWORK	A Number of alters (absolute size)	B Number of relationships among alters	C Maximum number of relationships possible*	D Density $D = (B \div C) \times 100$	E Redundancy $E = (2 \times B) \div A$	F Effective Size $F = A - E$
Q1. Talking about important matters						
Q2. Work-related communication						
Q3. Project support						
Q4. Informal socializing						

*The maximum number of relationships possible (C) depends on the number of alters (A). Use the following table to obtain the entry for column C.

If the number of alters (A) is . . .	Then the maximum number of relationships possible (C) is . . .
1	(undefined)
2	1
3	3
4	6
5	10

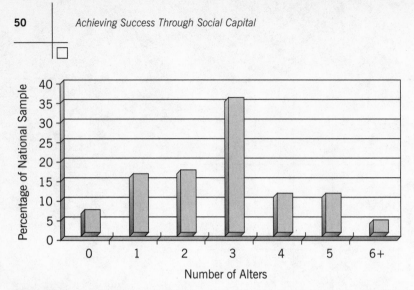

Figure 2.3. Number of People with Whom Respondent (Ego) Talks About Important Matters, General Social Survey

Composition

So far, you've looked at the size and structure of your networks. The next topic is the *composition,* the demographic characteristics of the people in your networks: age, education, gender, and race or ethnicity. How diverse or similar are the people you described in Worksheet 2.2? Referring to Worksheet 2.2, consider the similarity or diversity of the people in your networks along each demographic dimension. Indicate your answers on Worksheet 2.5.

Age. Are most people about your age, give or take five years? Then your networks are very similar with respect to age. Is there a spread of ages, so that some of the people you named are younger than this age bracket, and some are older? Then your networks are diverse with respect to this demographic characteristic. Generally, Americans' egocentric networks (based on Question 1 in Worksheet 2.1) are homogeneous with respect to age, compared with the heterogeneity of ages in the population as a whole.[28] Nonetheless, there is a high degree of variation: about a quarter of Americans have extremely homogeneous networks concentrated within a narrow band of ages, but another quarter have extremely diverse networks spanning a broad range of ages.[29]

Education. What is the distribution of formal education in your networks? Do most people fall in your category? If so, then your networks are homogeneous with respect to education. If they are spread across these categories, your networks are diverse with respect to this dimension. Thirty percent of Americans' egocentric networks (based on Question 1 in Worksheet 2.1) are extremely homogeneous with respect to education.[30]

Gender. Are all or most of the people in your networks the same gender as you? Or is there a mix of men and women? Maximum diversity occurs along this dimension when half of the people are men, and half are women. Only 22 percent of Americans have egocentric networks (based on Question 1 in Worksheet 2.1) that are composed entirely of the same gender; 37 percent have very diverse networks with respect to gender.[31]

Race or ethnicity. To what extent are the people in your networks spread across the categories listed for race or ethnicity? If they are mostly in one or two categories, then your networks are homogeneous along this dimension. If they are spread across categories, then your networks are diverse. This is the dimension of diversity that reveals the highest level of homogeneity: Over 90 percent of Americans have egocentric networks (based on Question 1 in Worksheet 2.1) that are composed entirely of the same race or ethnicity.[32]

(Note: The race or ethnicity categories in Worksheet 2.5 are those most commonly used in America. The appropriate categories depend, of course, on your national context. If you live outside the United States, edit the category labels to suit your context.)

■ Worksheet 2.5. Analyzing the Composition of Your Networks ■	
Demographic Characteristic	Percent of Alters
AGE	
Younger than you by 6 years or more	
Your age, plus or minus 5 years	
Older than you by 6 years or more	
	100 percent
FORMAL EDUCATION	
Less formal education than you	
Same formal education as you	
More formal education than you	
	100 percent
GENDER	
Male	
Female	
	100 percent
RACE or ETHNICITY	
Asian	
Black or African American	
Hispanic	
White	
Other (not listed here)	
	100 percent

Generally, diversity is more important than size. Recall, for example, that the diversity of a network is what protects against the common cold, not the size of a network (as described in the case study in Chapter One). Of course, the size of a network is not entirely unimportant. Having no customers is the death knell for a business; having no or few confidants is a prescription for unhappiness. One of five Americans, for example, talks with only one person about important matters—or doesn't talk with anyone at all (see Figure 2.3). Such networks are much too small to provide adequate social support, according to experts.[33]

Diversity provides the benefits of multiple perspectives on problems, protection against groupthink, and enhanced ability to collect, process, and digest information. Management teams with members from diverse functional backgrounds, for example, perform better than homogeneous management teams.[34] Diversity matters because it is often correlated with network size and structure. As a rule, small and closed networks are homogeneous; large and open networks are diverse.[35] For example, I would predict that Sue's network (Figure 2.2) is more diverse than Bill's. This might not be true along every dimension of composition, but the general tendency applies to most networks. Further, similar people tend to have similar networks. Consequently, if your networks are composed of similar people, it's likely that their egocentric networks coincide. They fold back on each other, and your larger network is more likely to be like Bill's. If your networks are composed of diverse types of people, it's likely that their egocentric networks don't coincide. They reach into different parts of the world instead of folding back; your larger network is more likely to be like Sue's, and you're likely to enjoy the same advantages that Sue does.

Focus

The last dimension, focus, tells you the extent to which your networks are concentrated in certain areas, activities, or interests.

It's useful to consider three areas of focus: work versus family, global versus domestic, and outside affiliation. Refer to Worksheet 2.2 for your description of the people in your networks, and to Worksheet 2.3 for your affiliations. Record your responses in Worksheet 2.6.

Work versus family. If most of the relationships in your networks are work-related, then your focus is work; if most of the relationships involve family, then your focus is family. Considering the people you described in Worksheet 2.2, what is the distribution of work alters, family alters, and other types? A little more than half of the alters in the average American's egocentric network are family members and other relatives, based on Question 1 in Worksheet 2.1.[36]

Global versus domestic. If all or most of the people you named have significant experience living or working abroad, then your networks are global; if most do not, then your networks are domestic. Considering the people you described in Worksheet 2.2, what is the distribution of those with global versus domestic experience? Almost 85 percent of the networks of the American businesspeople I've examined via my work with HUMAX Corporation are domestic.

Affiliations. If you are actively involved with many types of outside associations, groups, and organizations, then your focus is external. If you are actively involved with few types of outside associations, groups, and organizations, then your focus is internal. Worksheet 2.3 lists ten possibilities. Count the total number of kinds of outside affiliations you have, and divide by 10 (the maximum possible) to calculate a percentage. Record the percentage on Worksheet 2.6. Is your level of involvement high or low? On average, Americans are involved with only two types of outside groups, associations, or organizations, according to the 1995–1997 World Values Surveys, which yields an involvement percentage of 2 divided by 10, or 20 percent.[37]

■ Worksheet 2.6. Analyzing the Focus of Your Networks ■	
Areas of Focus	Percent of Alters
WORK AND FAMILY FOCUS	
Work	
Family	
Other	
	100 percent
GLOBAL FOCUS	
Global	
Domestic	
	100 percent
AFFILIATION FOCUS	Percent of 10 Types of Affiliations
Actively involved	
Not actively involved	
	100 percent

The three areas of focus—work versus family, global versus domestic, and affiliation—tell you whether your networks are focused internally or externally. As you'll see in Chapter Three, networks naturally tend to become internally focused or concentrated around activities.[38] So, for example, if most of your alters are work-related, then your networks are internally focused on work activities. If most of your alters are family-related, then your networks are internally focused on family life. The most internally focused networks of all include an exclusive focus on work or family, a highly domestic focus, and a few out-side affiliations. The most externally focused networks are the opposite: a balanced focus on work and family, a highly global focus, and many types of outside affiliations. This second combination, I've found, is uncommon. Most networks are more internally than externally focused.

■ What Kind of Social Capital Do You Have?

The diagnosis of your networks provides clues. Now's the time to pull everything together and figure out what the clues reveal about the patterns and tendencies of your larger networks. This last step in the evaluation requires good judgment on your part. Only you can be the final judge of how well the egocentric sample represents your larger network.

Your diagnosis considers the three dimensions of your networks just discussed: size, composition, and focus.

The size, composition, and focus of your networks suggest the type of social capital available to you. To anchor your understanding of networks, consider the two poles of the social capital spectrum. At one pole there are small, closed, homogeneous, internally focused networks. These networks typically represent social capital in the form of trust and cooperation among a tight network of very similar people. These networks are good for building group loyalty, identity, and a sense of common purpose.[39] They may be inadequate, however, for getting information or other resources, or for influencing people outside the networks. They are subject to groupthink and the development of an us-versus-them view of the world.

At the other pole there are large, open, diverse, externally focused networks. These are entrepreneurial networks in the extreme because the absence of connections among alters—what I earlier called "connections among connections"—represents social capital in the form of numerous opportunities to create value by bridging gaps—that is, by closing "structural holes" between people.[40] These entrepreneurial networks are excellent for getting lots of new information, learning about new opportunities, and finding resources. Due to the lack of connections among connections, however, these networks are not so good for building consensus, producing consistent expectations, or developing a sense of common mission; they may be prone to conflicts and tensions.[41]

The Networks of a Successful Entrepreneur

Let's examine a case between these two poles, the networks of Thomas Caprel. Tom is a venture capitalist and founder of Caprel Consulting, a midsized computer services firm in suburban Chicago. He is a successful entrepreneur who has built networks that strike a good balance for him in his work and personal lives. Nonetheless, the results of his evaluation showed some areas for development. He used the diagnosis as his guide for building his networks. Later in this chapter I will describe some of the changes he made.

Dimension 1: Effective Size. The sociograms of Tom's four networks and some of the statistics from Worksheet 2.4 are shown in Figure 2.4. Recall that five is the maximum number of alters allowed per question; twenty is the maximum for the entire sociometric survey. Tom named five alters for each of two questions (discussions about important matters and informal socializing), and four alters for each of the two other questions (work-related communications and project support). In sum, he had eighteen responses across the four survey questions. But the total number of *unique* names is smaller, because Tom has some overlap in his networks. Some alters appear more than once—Roger, Susan, Harry, and Alex. In my experience, almost every person who completes a sociometric survey such as the one included in this chapter or the online HUMAX Assessment has some overlap. But the amount of overlap in Tom's networks is lower than the average. In particular, his sociograms show that his work and social networks are rather separate.

Q1. Discussions about important matters

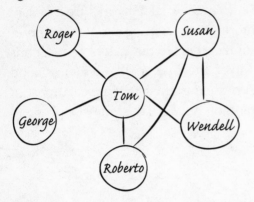

Number of alters = 5
Effective size = 3.8
Density = 30%

Q2. Work-related communications

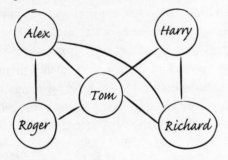

Number of alters = 4
Effective size = 2.5
Density = 50%

Q3. Project support

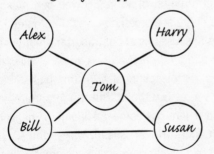

Number of alters = 4
Effective size = 3
Density = 33%

Figure 2.4. Picturing Tom Caprel's Egocentric Networks: Four Sociograms

Q4. Informal socializing

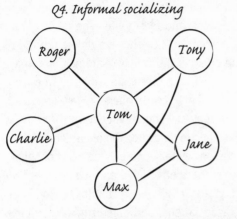

Number of alters = 5
Effective size = 4.2
Density = 20%

Figure 2.4. Picturing Tom Caprel's Egocentric Networks (cont.)

The structure of Tom's networks indicates substantial social capital in the form of entrepreneurial opportunities. His four egocentric networks contain many structural holes. Most of the alters in Tom's networks are not connected to each other. You can see the lack of connections among alters in his sociograms, as well as in the summary measures of effective size and density. Tom's networks are sparse, compared to most networks I've evaluated. All indicators point to the same conclusion: His networks contain many entrepreneurial opportunities. The structure of his egocentric networks suggests that he has good networking reach into the larger world of networks.

Dimension 2: Composition. The people in Tom's networks are diverse in most respects. When he analyzed the composition of his networks, using Worksheet 2.5, he saw that his networks contain a considerable span of ages and levels of formal education. His networks are relatively homogenous with respect to gender, however, and they are racially homogeneous. (Racial homogeneity is typical of the networks of most Americans, according to the General Social Survey.[42]) Therefore, the overall composition of Tom's networks falls in the middle of the diversity scale. The composition of his networks indicates that he reaps the benefits of diversity, but that he would be able to create more value by diversifying his contacts.

Dimension 3: Focus. Most networks, I've found, focus solely on work; some show a balance of work and family life. The results from Tom's analysis of focus, using Worksheet 2.6, shows a different pattern: the majority (54 percent) of the alters in his networks are neither family-related nor work-related. These include professional advisers, a coach/mentor, and friends. Thirty percent of his thirteen alters are family-related, while about 15 percent are work-related. Fifteen percent may seem low, but it reflects Tom's leadership style: He delegates the operational details to his managers, so he can focus on strategy and external relationships.

About 40 percent of Tom's alters have lived and worked in other countries, giving his networks an above-average global focus. Tom's affiliations with outside groups, associations, and organizations span five of the ten types listed in Worksheet 2.3. These four types include two professional associations (which count as one type), an industry group, a cultural organization, a sports and recreation club, and a personal development group. This is much higher than the average of two types of outside affiliations for the typical American.[43]

Summary. Tom's profile falls between the two social capital extremes, but it is closer to the high end of each dimension of social capital. His networks are a balance of the strengths and weaknesses of the two forms of social capital, but they *favor* the entrepreneurial end of the spectrum. His networks are typical of a successful entrepreneur.

Source: This case study is related to an analysis of Tom Caprel's social capital in which I diagnosed his networks using the Web-administered HUMAX Assessment. This was published in the Mastering Strategy series of the *Financial Times* (November 1999), "Networks: Building Social Capital as an Organizational Competence." The complete article is available in the "Articles" section of the HUMAX Web site at http://www.HUMAXnetworks.com.

What type of social capital do you have? Compare your results with Tom's. If your networks are substantially smaller, denser, less diverse, and more internally focused, then you likely have access to social capital in the form of trust and cooperation among a small group of people, but not to social capital in the form of entrepreneurial opportunities. If your networks are substantially larger, less dense, more diverse, and more externally focused than Tom's, then you likely have access to social capital in the form of entrepreneurial opportunities, but not to social capital in the form of trust and cooperation. If your networks are more or less the same as Tom's, then you may have a balance of the two forms of social capital, while favoring the entrepreneurial type.

What is the best? The "best" depends on fit with your purpose and context, as several sociologists and organizational theorists have noted.[44] No one type can fit all situations. For example, if your goal is to build a close-knit team with a common mission, consistent performance expectations, and a strong sense of common identity, then smaller, more homogeneous, more internally focused networks would serve your goal better than larger, more diverse, more externally focused networks. Conversely, if your goal is to get more information and discover new opportunities, the opposite is true. And remember that networks are dynamic: As your goals and needs change, you should manage your networks in a way that allows you to shift from one type toward the other and back again. For your purposes in this chapter, consider two fundamental conclusions from my research with HUMAX Corporation:

- *First, the extreme types are rare.* Most people fall somewhere between the pole of small, homogeneous, internally focused networks and the pole of large, diverse, externally focused networks.

- *Second, most networks fall closer to the low ends* than to the high ends of the dimensions of size, composition, and focus. Most networks tend to be small, homogeneous, and internally focused. Unlike Tom Caprel's networks, most networks I've diagnosed favor this pole rather than the entrepreneurial pole.

Therefore, after diagnosing their networks, most people conclude that they could benefit by enlarging, diversifying, and externalizing their networks. Their conclusions don't prescribe jumping completely to the entrepreneurial pole and attempting to build the largest, most diverse, most externally oriented networks possible. But moving in the direction of more entrepreneurial networks would help most people to be more effective and influential by getting more information, discovering more opportunities, being ready to find new roles in an organization or new jobs in the labor market, and being better prepared generally to cope with the uncertainties and ambiguities of today's business world. And, as you'll see in the next two chapters, building and using entrepreneurial networks enables you to create more value with your networks and to be of more service to others.

■ Accident or Strategy?

Why do your networks look the way they do? It's not because of your personality, especially if the nature of your work requires you to interact with others to get the job done. Consider, for example, the results of a study conducted by Ron Burt and his associates on the relationship between "entrepreneurial personality types" and "entrepreneurial networks."[45] Burt's group found that people with entrepreneurial personalities are more likely to build entrepreneurial networks *if* they work as clerks, technical types, or junior managers. In contrast, networks and personality are not related for middle and upper-level managers, who build entrepreneurial networks whether or not they have entrepreneurial personalities. Why? Clerks, technical types, and junior managers don't need to build entrepreneurial networks to get their jobs done. (Clerks can work alone if they want to; for example, they don't have business lunches with anyone.) As people move up the organization, however, they have less discretion: They *have to* build more entrepreneurial networks if they are going to be successful.

My consulting experience supports the conclusions of this research.[46] Personality is not destiny. Building networks is a skill;

anyone, regardless of personality, can improve their networks. For example, an executive at a major financial services firm told me that he consistently comes up as an "introvert" every time he takes the Myers-Briggs Type Indicator (a well-known diagnostic tool used for personality assessment). Yet he has larger, more diverse, and more externally focused networks than the average person in his firm. His profile looks a lot like Tom Caprel's. He is always "in the know" because his networks are so good; he creates value for the firm (and boosts his career) by finding and capitalizing on emerging opportunities. "I figured out early on," he told me, "that I had to build good networks if I was going to be successful." He did; he is. This executive made deliberate choice a big driver of the structure, composition, and focus of his networks.

For most people, however, the big driver of networks is not deliberate choice, it's *accident*. Most networks are accidents. They result from unthinking reactions to constraints rather than from deliberate strategies of how to add value by building networks. Some people let their networks shrink because their jobs are demanding and they don't conceive of different ways to do them. Others pass up natural opportunities to globalize their networks, such as the chance to take a temporary assignment abroad. And others pass up opportunities to diversify their networks by participating in a formal job rotation program or volunteering to serve on a multifunctional task force. What about your networks? For example, what produced your networks? Why aren't they smaller—or bigger? Why do they have these people in them, and not some other set of people? Why are people connected? These questions may seem odd, but figuring out why your networks look the way they do is critical for understanding social capital.

Constraint, opportunity, and choice are the three drivers of networks, the forces that produce the patterns and composition of networks. But these are not equal forces behind most networks. Most people, I've learned, let the accidents of constraint and opportunity create their networks; they don't choose their networks. The best networkers, however, make deliberate choice a big driver, like Tom Caprel and the financial services executive I just described.

Choice is the set of decisions you make about your networks—how you respond to constraints and opportunities. Often, implicit assumptions drive your choices. Some people assume that one should separate personal life from business life. For others, choices are driven by the *similarity principle*—the tendency to associate with people like oneself. What are your assumptions about networks?

Constraint is anything that creates barriers, limits, or pressures on your networks. For example, if you work in an all-male environment, chances are your networks are predominantly male. If your work requires you to put in long hours at the office, then your networks are probably focused on work. Common constraints are the demands of work, the size and type of organization in which one works, place of residence, and limited time or money.

Opportunity is any possibility that exists in your environment. For example, if your workplace includes equal numbers of men and women, then you have the opportunity to develop networks with gender diversity. If your own or your organization's resources enable you to travel to conferences, then you have the opportunity to meet different people from different places. If your neighborhood supports a local association, then you have the opportunity to meet and develop relationships with your neighbors. What opportunities do you have? Do you take advantage of them?

Use Worksheet 2.7 to help you analyze the drivers of your networks. For an illustration, consider two of Tom Caprel's responses to this exercise:

■ Worksheet 2.7. Analyzing the Drivers of Your Networks ■

	Network Drivers		
	What *constraints* drive my networks?	What *opportunities* drive my networks?	What *choices* drive my networks?
Dimension 1 Effective size of your networks			
Dimension 2 Composition of your networks			
Dimension 3 Focus of your networks			

The profile of my company and industry is young and male, and so was my network. So I began mentoring female executives through Menttium to expand my gender diversity.

As a CEO I often was starved for conversation and direction at the strategic level. Hence, I joined TEC to increase my accessibility to other CEOs and to get their assistance in making decisions. This also increases my diversity across industries.

The group Tom mentions, TEC, is a seven-thousand-member worldwide organization founded in 1957 to provide a peer forum and learning environment for company presidents, managing directors, and top executives. It includes a wide range of company sizes, from small entrepreneurial firms to large corporations. Each local group convenes monthly in a professionally facilitated meeting of executives from a diverse set of industries.

CHAPTER SUMMARY

Most people don't have an accurate fix on their social capital. That is, most people's casual perceptions of the extent to which their friends are friends are pretty inaccurate, and most people don't really understand the needs and wants of their spouses or close friends—even though they *believe* they do. That's the rub: Most people think they understand their networks, but most people really don't. Hence, most people benefit from using the sociometric techniques presented in this chapter.

The intent of the sociometric survey was to provide you with a sample of your larger networks, one that would give you clues to the state and quality of your social capital. People with small, homogeneous, internally focused networks typically experience social capital in the form of trust and cooperation within a tight network, but they lack the ability to get information or discover entrepreneurial opportunities. Those with large, diverse, externally focused networks typically have access to social capital in the form of entrepreneurial opportunities, but they also experience mixed messages, conflicting expectations, and tensions. Most networks fall between these two poles, but they *favor* the low ends of the three dimensions—small and closed, homogeneous composition, and narrowly inward focus. Most people discover that their networks are smaller, more homogeneous, and more internally focused than they imagined; most conclude that they should enlarge, diversify, and externalize their networks. This conclusion doesn't mean that they should build the most entrepreneurial networks possible, only that they should build networks more like Tom Caprel's, the successful entrepreneur described in this chapter.

The end of one journey is the beginning of another. The next chapter turns to what you can do to *build* your social capital. Because most people wish to make their networks more entrepreneurial, that is the focus of Chapter Three. As you'll see, by building these sorts of networks, you produce the kind of social capital that helps you to create more value, help more people, and make the world a more connected place.

Building Entrepreneurial Networks

t sounds silly, I know, but in years of hiking and mountaineering trips, I've learned that the hardest part of the journey can be finding the trailhead. Many times I've started down a trail, only to discover that it's the wrong one; I have to retrace my steps and start anew. Many mapmakers simply assume that hikers know where the trailhead is and need help only in finding the path to the summit.

I offer this tale as a metaphor of the importance of starting off in the right direction. The trailhead question for this book is, Social capital for what? *Why* do you want to build a better network? Once you address this question, you can continue your journey by considering the fundamental principle behind the operation of entrepreneurial networks—the universal "law of nature" that makes entrepreneurial networks work so well. With the answer to the trailhead question as a moral guide and this fundamental principle in hand, you'll take the last leg of your trek in this chapter, focusing specifically on what you can do to build your networks.

■ Social Capital for What?

I've conducted various sociometric exercises like the one in Chapter Two with over a thousand people.[1] As I mentioned there, most people conclude that their networks are too small, too homogeneous, too inwardly focused, and too much the result of accident rather than choice. They resolve to make their networks more entrepreneurial. When I get to this point during a social capital workshop, I ask, *Why*? Why do you want entrepreneurial networks? At first, the usual response is silence, accompanied by quizzical looks. Slowly, the discussion restarts, and participants offer reasons. Specifics vary, but the theme is the same: what one gets through networks—leads, sales, jobs, information, financial capital, emotional support, and so on.

These responses seem natural enough, but in fact the focus on getting isn't a good, powerful, or empowering reason for building better networks. Resources travel through networks, but fixating on what you get doesn't initiate their movement toward you. Paradoxically, the reverse is true: a focus on giving initiates the creation and circulation of resources that flow back to you. "If you want to go north, head south" is particularly relevant advice here.

Practitioners and philosophers alike promote the same ethic, if not always in the language of networks. The goal of building networks is to contribute to others. Doing it the other way around—to help oneself—is ultimately self-defeating. I can summon many and diverse sources to make the point, from biblical wisdom ("It is more blessed to give than receive") to the Chinese feng shui approach to networking (from a book given to me by my colleague Jim Walsh, who spotted it in a Hong Kong bookstore).[2] A mark of emotional maturity, say psychologists, is the switch from a focus on getting to the joy of giving. Consider the sage advice offered by networking experts Donna Fisher and Sandy Vilas:

> Networking consists of creating links from people we know to people they know in an organized way, for a specific purpose, while remaining committed to doing our part and expecting nothing in return. The key phrase here is the last part, "expecting nothing in return."
>
> Expecting nothing in return means giving, contributing to, and supporting others without keeping score. Keeping score blocks the flow and makes people hesitant to give in return. Think about how you feel when you know that others are keeping track of what they have done for you and what they in turn think you owe them. You probably feel less inclined to network with them. And if you are the one keeping score, your focus may be more on the score than the opportunity in front of you.[3]

Of course, a fixation on "getting" can produce results—in the short run. There is a science of manipulation, and one can learn how to use it. Psychologist Robert Cialdini studied the tactics used by those who know how to get others to do what they want. He describes the arsenal of "weapons of influence" wielded by con artists, swindlers, salespeople, fundraisers, peddlers, politicians, and other "compliance professionals."[4] For example, unethical sales trainers teach salespeople to "mirror and match" the attributes, body language, and verbal style of potential customers.[5] This tactic invokes the *liking principle*—the human tendency to comply with requests made by people we like—even if they're strangers. The bases of liking include physical attractiveness, similarity with one's attitudes, personality, lifestyle, religion, or demographic attributes, as well as compliments, cooperative behavior, and a person's association with good news.[6] Merely liking a seller increases the likelihood of a sale. So, if a new-car saleswoman spots a baby seat in your old car, she'll start talking about her children, even if she doesn't have any. A salesman in Michigan who notices a bumper sticker for the Detroit Redwings will talk about his love of hockey, even if he doesn't know the difference between a hockey puck and a Frisbee. If you curse, he'll pepper his speech with a few choice words, too.

My long-time friend and collaborator Rob Faulkner and I observed these manipulative practices in our research on financial fraud.[7] For example, one con artist bilked over $11 million from investors by manipulating "symbols of authority"[8] to show investors the appearance of credibility and success. The company had tony offices at a prestigious address; the president of the firm drove a black Lamborghini and a red Rolls Royce, and had twenty Bijan suits valued at $2,500 each. One victim told us that he decided to invest after he drove by the president's home and saw the Rolls Royce parked in front; another was persuaded after the president pointed out his office window to the Lamborghini parked below, saying, "Do you think I'd be driving a car like that if I wasn't successful?" (This authority symbol had been purchased with stolen funds.)

A cynic would argue that the swindler's manipulative networking tactics were successful; after all, even though he was morally corrupt, he accumulated over $11 million in financial capital. True. But if he had been honest, he could have amassed much more. Rob and I discovered that few investors referred the company to their social networks of friends, colleagues, and business associates. This absence of word-of-mouth publicity is unusual; most products and services—including investment opportunities—spread or *diffuse* through social networks.[9] This is the "diffusion effect" marketers dream of. Why didn't it happen? We asked a large sample of investors. Here's what they said: They sensed that something was wrong, out of place; something didn't seem right. Their uneasiness didn't stop them from investing, but it did stop them from roping in their friends, family, and colleagues. Without knowing it, the suspicious investors blocked the word-of-mouth diffusion effect on which legitimate businesses thrive.

Consider another story, a bit more mundane. Once, in Chicago, a pickpocket lifted my wife's purse, found our new ATM card and PIN, and promptly withdrew $300 from our checking account, the maximum withdrawal allowed in a twenty-four-hour period. We reported the stolen ATM card within hours and it was deactivated. I thought that there was some limit to the amount we would be liable for, but our banker disavowed any such notion, saying that we were responsible for the full amount of any unauthorized withdrawals. After all, our personal banker said, it was our fault and we should be liable for the total loss. However, he would be "fair" and split the difference. The bank lost $150, we lost $150. Even though we accepted his settlement, we both felt something was amiss. Later, we learned that there is a law governing the unauthorized use of an ATM card, the Electronic Fund Transfer Act (EFTA). If you report a lost or stolen card before it is used, the card issuer can't hold you responsible for any monetary loss. If it's used before you report it, but you call within two business days, the card issuer can't hold you responsible for more than $50. This was our situation, but we had forfeited our rights by accepting the banker's offer. Our personal banker had deceived us for short-term gain. What else might happen, we wondered? Could we trust our banker in the future? Or would we have to consult our attorney every time we negotiated with him, just to make sure we knew our rights? We talked it over and decided to close all our accounts. When new colleagues moved to the area, I advised them to avoid this bank. I also told my students about the experience. You can be sure that the bank lost more than $150.

Both stories illustrate the same principle: Manipulative, dishonest, deceptive, or deceitful tactics don't work in the long run. In the first story, a fraudulent business was denied the power of word-of-mouth marketing; in the second, an unethical practice generated negative word of mouth, losing current and future customers. Bad news travels faster through the networks than good news!

The point applies to all kinds of getting behavior, not just blatantly unethical or illegal tactics. People come equipped with sensitive antennae for manipulative practices; they can tell if the real focus is getting and not giving; they bristle when they sense that a "technique" is being used on them. Lack of authenticity and sincere interest in others betrays itself in all kinds of behaviors—trying to make a sale in a first meeting, superficial conversations, not taking time to establish genuine rapport, feigning interest, listening to get rather than to give, and so on.[10] Even if people do business with you, they won't go out of their way to help you in return. And they won't tap you into the hidden resources in their networks. You only need to think about your reactions when other people try manipulative practices on you to know how true this is.

It's hard to relinquish the focus on getting. It's rooted deep in the modern individualist culture. Once you learn to hold it in abeyance, however, you can view new possibilities. New research on the psychology of human development suggests grand possibilities for networks. The premise of many traditional psychological theories is *gratification:* at bottom, according to these theories, people strive to fulfill innate self-centered "drives." The new theories argue that the primary motivation is *participation:* growth and development in connection with others. This is the foundation of the "relational practice" perspective, developed by Jean Baker Miller, Irene Pierce Stiver, and others.[11] As Viktor Frankl argued, happiness eludes us if we pursue it directly. Rather, it's participation in meaningful relationships and activities that leads to happiness, growth, and satisfaction. "Achieving meaningful participation in one's culture and society," says Barton Hirsch, "is an important task confronting us throughout our lives."[12] Social networks, Hirsch says, reflect our involvement in life.

Whether viewed from a moral perspective or in down-to-earth pragmatic terms, the ultimate purpose of building better networks is to enhance participation in relationships with others. Through networks, we make our contributions to the world. The joy of participation and contribution is one of the "hidden resources" in every network.

■ The Small-World Principle

Psychologist Kurt Lewin's wise dictum, "There's nothing as practical as a good theory," applies to building networks. One of those good, practical theories is the *small-world principle*. It provides deep insights into the way the world is organized, and why entrepreneurial networks work. Understanding the theory improves one's ability to build better networks: the *why* powers the *how*.

Here's a little question to introduce the theory . . .

Who Is the Center of the Universe?

You might be surprised. Putting aside major and minor deities, the center of the universe is the film actor Kevin Bacon. You know Kevin. He was in *Sleepers* (1996), *Apollo 13* (1995), *The River Wild* (1994), *A Few Good Men* (1992), *JFK* (1991), *He Said, She Said* (1991), *Flatliners* (1990), *Tremors* (1990), *Footloose* (1984), *Diner*

(1982), *Friday the 13th* (1980), and *Animal House* (1978)—just to name a few of the more than forty feature films in which he appeared.

How do you know that Kevin is the Center of the Universe? The only way to know the answer to such a grand question is to consult an oracle. Fortunately, there is one: The Oracle of Bacon at Virginia, a Web site hosted by the Department of Computer Science, School of Engineering, at the University of Virginia, Charlottesville. The Oracle is open to any pilgrim with a computer and Web browser (http://www.cs.virginia.edu/oracle/). If your quest takes you to the Oracle of Bacon, you will learn that every actress or actor has a "Bacon Number." A Bacon Number indicates how close the person is to the Center of the Universe. Kevin has a Bacon Number of 0, of course. Anyone who worked on a film with Kevin has a Bacon Number of 1. Anyone who worked on a film with someone who worked on a film with Kevin has a Bacon Number of 2. A Bacon Number of 3? That's anyone who worked on a film with someone who worked on a film with someone who worked on a film with Kevin. And so on and so on, until you find the unlucky few who are not connected to Kevin by chains of any length, no matter how long (their Bacon Numbers are infinity). Try your hand at guessing these Bacon Numbers:

Sarah Jessica Parker's Bacon Number is _____.
Ronald Reagan's Bacon Number is _____.
Charlie Chaplin's Bacon Number is _____.

Check the footnote for the answers.* Surprised? Most people are. In turns out that it's very difficult to get a large Bacon

---

*Bacon numbers for Parker, Reagan, and Chaplin: 1, 2, 3. Sarah Jessica Parker was in *Footloose* (1984) with Bacon. Ronald Reagan was in *Brother Rat* (1938) with Eddie Albert, who was in *The Big Picture* (1989) with Bacon. Charlie Chaplin was in *Monsieur Verdoux* (1947) with Barry Norton, who was in *What Price Glory* (1952) with Robert Wagner, who was in *Wild Things* (1988) with Bacon. If you consult the Oracle enough, you'll discover that Robert Wagner often appears in chains connecting actors and actresses to Kevin. He is a "funnel" in the small world.

Number. After all, Kevin is the Center of the Universe. Visit the Oracle and see if you can find chains with more than six links. (If you find a longer chain, your name will be enshrined in the Oracle's Hall of Fame.) Try obscure actors, foreign-film actresses, even adult-movie stars—anyone you think would be far from the center. You'll see that everyone is connected to Kevin by surprisingly short chains. (The reason why is a clue for later.) Here is the Oracle's Table of Bacon Numbers, showing Kevin's connections to 360,805 actors and actresses:[13]

Table 3.1. Table of Bacon Numbers

Bacon Number	Film Actors and Actresses
0	1
1	1,426
2	97,114
3	212,118
4	47,182
5	2,641
6	257
7	64
8	2

I should mention that the Oracle, a stickler for accuracy, tells you that, in fact, 668 other actors and actresses are more "central" than Kevin Bacon. Sean Connery is one, with an average "Connery Number" of 2.64, compared with an average Bacon number of 2.86. But, as #669 out of over 300,000 actors and actresses, Kevin is in the top 1 percent. (Rod Steiger is the "true" Center of the Hollywood universe, but this is, after all, the Oracle of Bacon.)[14]

Consider now an entirely different universe, mathematics, and the story of its center, Paul Erdös (1913–1996), a brilliant, eccentric, and prodigiously prolific mathematician.[15] Mathematics has Erdös Numbers, just as Hollywood has Bacon Numbers. Paul has an Erdös Number of 0. Anyone who coauthored a paper with Paul has an Erdös Number of 1 (there are 472). A mathematician who coauthored a paper with someone who coauthored a paper with Paul has an Erdös Number of 2, and so on, just like the Bacon series. How close a mathematician is to Paul is a mark of status in the math community: the smaller the Erdös Number, the higher the status of the holder of the number. Status is serious business. Mathematicians put their Erdös Numbers on their résumés and curriculum vitae!

How did Paul get to be the center of the mathematical universe? In his eighty-three years, he authored or coauthored over fifteen hundred academic papers on a diverse range of math topics. Yet it wasn't his sheer volume as much as his mode of operation that put Paul in the center. (This is another clue you'll pick up in a moment.) As Paul Hoffman describes in his 1998 biography, *The Man Who Loved Only Numbers:*

> Erdös (pronounced "air-dish") structured his life to maximize the amount of time he had for mathematics. He had no wife or children, no job, no hobbies, not even a home, to tie him down. He lived out of a shabby suitcase and a drab orange plastic bag from Centrum Aruhaz ("Central Warehouse"), a large department store in Budapest [his birthplace]. In a never-ending search for good mathematical problems and fresh mathematical talent, Erdös crisscrossed four continents at a frenzied pace, moving from one university or research center to the next. His modus operandi was to show up on the doorstep of a fellow mathematician, declare, "My brain is open," work with his host for a day or two, until he was bored or his host was run down, and then move on to another home.
>
> Erdös's motto was not "Other cities, other maidens" but "Another roof, another proof." He did mathematics in more than 25 different countries, completing proofs in remote places and sometimes publishing them in equally obscure journals.[16]

There are centers of all the known universes. Consider the world of Chicago, the third-largest city in the nation. Who do you suppose the center is? Mayor Richard M. Daley? Former Chicago Bulls superstar Michael Jordan? Good guesses, but the true Center of Chicago is Lois Weisberg, a seventy-three-year-old grandmother. As I write this, Lois is Commissioner of Cultural Affairs for the City of Chicago and an adviser to the mayor. Malcolm Gladwell chronicled her life and times as the center of Chicago networks in a *New Yorker* piece, "Six Degrees of Lois Weisberg."[17] Lois is the rare person who seems to know everybody—someone who can put you in touch with just about anyone else. No one has calculated the table of Weisberg Numbers, but I'm sure it's similar to Kevin Bacon's: thousands upon thousands of people connected via very short chains to Lois Weisberg.

How did Lois become the center of her universe? She has lived and worked and hung out in many different contexts; she has championed a variety of causes; she has lived her life in a way that bridges diverse and isolated worlds. As Gladwell explains,

> If you go through [her] history and keep count, the number of worlds that Lois has belonged to comes to eight: the actors, the writers, the doctors, the lawyers, the park lovers, the politicians, the railroad buffs, and the flea-market aficionados. When I asked Lois to make her own list, she added musicians and the visual artists and architects and hospitality-industry people whom she works with in her current job. But if you look harder at Lois's life you could probably subdivide her experiences into fifteen or twenty worlds. She has the same ability to move among different subcultures and niches that the busiest actors do.[18]

To illustrate the universality of the small-world principle, here is one more example. From movies and mathematics and civic mavens we go to the rarified universe of corporations and their boards of directors. My colleague Jerry Davis at the University of Michigan has mapped the universe of corporate boards, examining the "interlock network" of the thousand largest corporations in America and their ten thousand corporate directors. (An "interlock" occurs when one director serves on two corporate boards.)

Who's the center of the corporate universe? None other than Vernon Jordan, President Clinton's friend and confidant. How does Jerry know Jordan is the center? Jerry ranked all ten thousand directors by centrality in the interlock network. Jordan came out #1.

How did Jordan get to be the center? It isn't his connection to President Clinton, any more than Lois Weisberg's connection to the mayor of Chicago is the source of her centrality. Vernon, a lawyer by training, began his career as a civil rights activist. For years, he headed the Urban League; in 1999 he was a senior partner in the Washington, D.C., office of the law (lobbyist) firm Akin, Gump, Strauss, Hauer & Feld, L.L.P. In 1972, Jordan was invited to join the board of directors of Bankers Trust; one year later, he joined J.C. Penney's board. Since then, he has become a director of a host of American corporate icons, including Xerox, American Express, Dow Jones, J.C. Penney, Revlon, Union Carbide, Ryder Systems, and Sara Lee, as well as prestigious nonprofits such as the Ford Foundation, Howard University, National Academy Foundation, and the Roy Wilkins Foundation. By virtue of his diverse board memberships, he connects disparate companies, industries, and the for-profit and nonprofit sectors. The boards he connects are central boards, too, linking him via short chains to virtually all other boards. Thus Vernon Jordan is central in the same way Lois Weisberg is central, or Paul Erdös or Kevin Bacon: he spans diverse and isolated regions of the world.

The Small-World Phenomenon

Bacon, Erdös, Weisberg, and Jordan—a motley crew with one fundamental feature in common: By connecting regions of the world, each one creates the well-known "small-world phenomenon." As mathematician Duncan Watts defines it,

> The small-world phenomenon formalises the anecdotal notion that "you are only ever 'six degrees of separation' away from

anyone else on the planet." Almost everyone is familiar with the sensation of running into a complete stranger at a party or in some public arena and, after a short conversation, discovering that they know somebody unexpected in common. "Well, it's a small world!" they exclaim. The small-world phenomenon is a generalised version of this experience. The claim being that even when two people do not have a friend in common, they are separated by only a short chain of intermediaries.[19]

This familiar experience was captured in the movie *Six Degrees of Separation* and the play on which it was based. Six degrees seems like a very short chain. But you might be surprised to know that this is a *long* chain, given the arithmetic of networks. Suppose each person has, on average, about a thousand acquaintances.[20] That might seem like a large number, but it's a conservative estimate; the typical professional, for example, is acquainted with over thirty-five hundred people. If each of a thousand acquaintances *also* has a thousand acquaintances, and the pattern of acquaintanceships is random, then the average "degrees of separation" between any two people in the United States should be only *two* links!

So why wasn't the movie titled *Two Degrees of Separation*? The reason is that networks are not random at all; they are highly patterned. The world is divided up and organized into groups on the basis of age, education, geography, proximity, race, socioeconomic class, occupation, status, formal authority, and so forth. These dimensions dice society into clumps of similar people, with plenty of "white space" between these homogeneous clumps. These clumps may have fuzzy boundaries (that is, clumps can overlap), but the clumping effect is universal.

There are many reasons why people clump. Networks tend to form around activities and places. Sociologist Scott Feld calls this the "focused organization" of social networks. As he defines it, a focus is "a social, psychological, legal, or physical entity around which joint activities are organized (e.g., work places, voluntary organizations, hangouts, families, etc.)."[21] Residential zoning, for example, creates local communities with people of similar socioeconomic class, occupation, age, or race. (Consider, for instance, the age-homogeneous communities formed by the requirement in Arizona retirement villages that residents be at least fifty-five years old.) Within organizations and institutions, organizational design creates formal clumps, focusing networks within functions, departments, or divisions. These harden into the well-known functional silos in organizations—tall barriers to interaction and cooperation across functions. The demands of work and family often limit people's networks to these two spheres of life. Generally speaking, people tend to associate with others like themselves. This "similarity principle" is a powerful driver of human interaction.[22] For these and other reasons, networks are prone to form *within* clumps, not between them.

Clumpiness means that networks tend to fold back on themselves. For example, friends of friends tend to be friends. Indeed, having two friends who are not friends causes tension and conflict; sociologist Mark Granovetter calls this the "forbidden triad" because it is so unlikely to be sustained, due to the natural pressures for closure in the three-person friendship triangle.[23] This folding-back phenomenon is related to the "redundancy" factor I discussed in Chapter Two. Recall the illustration of Bill's and Sue's egocentric networks. Bill's network has a lot of redundancy in it: most of the people he connects are also connected to each other. So his network tends to fold back on itself, reinforcing a clump of densely interconnected people. In contrast, Sue's network exhibits much less redundancy. Only two people in her egocentric network are connected directly to each other, and so her networks extend out into the world instead of folding back on themselves. Her egocentric network *bridges* clumps. If more people had networks like Sue's—more bridges across clumps—then the average degree of separation would be fewer than six. But most people have networks like Bill's, creating clumps rather than bridging them. Clumping, then, is the reason you don't see two degrees of separation; the clumping of networks increases the average chain length to six links.

If most people live and work in clumps, what creates the small-world effect? The answer is people like Kevin Bacon, Paul Erdös, Lois Weisberg, and Vernon Jordan. How do these people make the big world small? They do it by serving as what Duncan Watts calls "linchpins" in the networks of the world.[24] By linking diverse clumps, they provide the shortcuts that convert a big world into a small one. Without them, the world would be a very big place—all clumps with no bridges, or at best, very long routes from one clump to another.

Watts identifies different types of linchpins. *Temporal linchpins* tie people across time and generations; an example is the veteran actor Eddie Albert, who made over eighty films in a sixty-year career. *Cultural linchpins* connect diverse ethnic cultures, such as martial artist Jackie Chan, who brings together Asian and American filmmakers. *Genre linchpins* link diverse categories, such as Mel Gibson, who links lowbrow action films like *Lethal Weapon* with highbrow art like *Hamlet*). To Watts's list I add *geographic linchpins,* who create shortcuts between far-apart communities. A good example is an acquaintance of mine, Ed Vielmetti, who is a consulting engineer for Cisco Systems, the world's leading provider of routers, switches, dial-up access servers, and other products that link computer networks and drive the Internet. Ed's clients are spread all over the country, so he could live almost anywhere. He chooses to make his home in Ann Arbor, Michigan, where he attended the University of Michigan, but he works at least one week a month at Cisco's headquarters in San Jose, California. Similarly, Eric Schmidt, CEO since March 1997 of software company Novell, makes his home in California's Silicon Valley though the company is headquartered in Utah. The continental United States is made small by people like Ed Vielmetti and Eric Schmidt.

Consider the four big worlds of feature films, mathematics, Chicagoland, and corporations, and how each linchpin makes it small:

- *Feature films.* The world of filmmaking is "big" because most actors or actresses make only one film, and most of those who make more than one film are typecast. One reason Kevin Bacon is a linchpin is that he's a character actor: He plays many different *types* of roles. He links the clumps of typecast actors who play the same roles again and again. If he were typecast like, say, Sylvester Stallone or John Wayne, Kevin could still have acted in lots of films, but he might not have become the center of his universe. By virtue of diversity, he bridges isolated and distant clumps of typecast actors and actresses.

- *Mathematics.* Solitary toil in an ivory tower is the typical academic work style. This style produces great works, but it also creates a big world of academics working alone or in small clumps (called "departments"). Paul Erdös was a linchpin because he practiced a collaborative, peripatetic work style, traveling the globe, doing math in twenty-five different countries, and coauthoring papers with over four hundred mathematicians along the way. By doing so, he linked otherwise isolated and distant clumps of mathematicians around the world. If Paul had adopted the typical work style of mathematicians he would still have been a prolific producer of math proofs, but he wouldn't have become the center of his universe, and the global community of mathematicians would be a lot bigger.

- *Chicagoland.* Over 8 million people live in Chicago's metropolitan area. Chicago is one of the most diverse cities in the world; virtually every ethnic group in America is represented there. Spanish and Polish, for example, are heard almost as often as English. Lois Weisberg makes this big city a lot smaller by linking together Chicago's many and diverse worlds. Her entrepreneurial networks span the worlds of actors, musicians, writers, architects, railroad lovers, flea-market habitues, jewelry shop owners, doctors, lawyers, park lovers, and politicians—to name a few. *New Yorker* writer Malcolm Gladwell concludes that Lois (and people like her) actually "run the world"—"I don't mean they are the sort who head up the Fed or General Motors or Microsoft, but that, in a very down-to-earth, day-to-day way, they make the world work. They spread ideas and information. They connect varied and isolated parts of society."[25] Chicago is called "the city that works." Lois is one reason why it does.

▪ *Corporations.* A board of directors sits on top of every public corporation in America. It can be lonely up there: Of the six thousand directors of the Fortune 500, only 8 percent get invited to sit on more than one board.[26] Corporate boards, therefore, are clumpy regions of the business world. They are connected by only a few people—like Vernon Jordan—who have entrepreneurial networks that interlock multiple boards. And keep in mind that Jordan is unusual: Few of the 8 percent of directors with multiple board memberships serve on as many boards as he does. The lonely world of corporate boards would be even lonelier if it weren't for linchpins like him. And it would be a more hostile place, too. A company with a well-connected board of directors is less likely to be swallowed in a hostile takeover attempt. Directors learn about new takeover defense tactics from the information flowing through the interlock network.

Linchpins spread ideas, information, and resources. They are the gateways between clumps. Without them, resources still might flow between clumps, but would take much longer; more likely, they would get stuck in a clump and never get out. Job seekers and job providers often live in different clumps. How do they find each other? Linchpins. Entrepreneurs and venture capitalists operate in different worlds. How do start-ups find angel or VC money? Linchpins. A problem arises in one department of an organization and its solution exists in another department. How do problems and solutions link up? Linchpins. How do consumers hear about new products and services? Linchpins.

I could go on, but the point is this: everyone's actions create a distribution of "numbers" in the world, just like the distributions of Bacon Numbers, Erdös Numbers, or Jordan Numbers. Everyone in the world has a "Baker Number" (how close they are to me), just as everyone in the world has a number with respect to you. Everyone's ability to find resources—of whatever kind—is a function of these "numbers," how close or far they are to these resources. Building an entrepreneurial network makes *you* a linchpin in your world. It's the way to cultivate the lucky "spiderweb" networks described in Chapter One. It's the way to find any resource you need—jobs, good people for jobs, innovative ideas, financial capital, new opportunities, and so on. Entrepreneurial networks are the structures that enable the creation of value for customers, clients, friends, family, employers, and communities. They are the vehicles enabling all of us to make our contributions to the world.

■ Making Your World Small: Building Entrepreneurial Networks

From the four stories in the preceding section—and a vast amount of scientific research—it is possible to deduce two corollary principles to the small-world idea that can serve as guides for building entrepreneurial networks. These corollary principles appear to be universally true of networks. Not only do they describe the organization of the social world, they even apply to the structure of neural (brain) networks and the power grid of the western United States![27]

1. *The world is clumpy.* The world is organized into regions of densely interconnected people or organizations. Most people live and work inside clumps; most personal, professional, and business networks are focused in clumps.

2. *A few shortcuts across the clumps create the small-world effect.* Duncan Watts estimates that as few as 1 percent of all ties need be shortcuts to create the effect. All it takes is a few well-traveled people, a few actors with diverse film credits, a few eccentric, peripatetic mathematicians, and so on.

Which type are you? Are you a clumper or a linchpin? Look back at your results from Chapter Two. Do the patterns in your self-diagnosis reveal clumping tendencies (like Bill's network) or linking tendencies (like Sue's network)? Or are you a third possibility: a loner going it alone? I've been all three at different times in my life. I grew up in a family of loners, clumped in a small semirural Connecticut village. Many years later I was a happy clumper with my fellow graduate students at Northwestern University, concentrating on our studies in a closed community of like-minded scholars. This was a wonderful phase of life; our networks were closed, but our minds were opened. This phase illustrates that clumping has its place; sometimes it is appropriate and necessary to clump. But when it came time to finish my doctoral studies and find a *job*, I needed to bridge different worlds: the job I wanted was not in the world I lived in, the Evanston suburb of Chicago. I found a good job with a consulting firm in Washington, D.C., via a linchpin I met—accidentally—on a Saturday morning in Evanston. (It's a long story, but you'll appreciate the serendipitous nature of the encounter when I tell you that it involved moving a used upright piano.) Since then, I have clumped again, but I always strive to build wider, more entrepreneurial networks, and to help whomever I can by linking together otherwise disconnected people, groups, and organizations.

You don't have to be a superlinchpin like Kevin Bacon or Vernon Jordan to invoke the small-world effect. My colleague Karl Weick promotes the concept of "small wins" as the embodiment of wisdom. The wisdom of small wins comes from other quarters as well, conveying the heart and spirit of the networking enterprise. Consider Edward Hallowell's prescription in *Connect: Twelve Vital Ties That Open Your Heart, Lengthen Your Life, and Deepen Your Soul:*

> Everyone can make a number of little changes that can deepen the connections in their lives. For example, you can get in touch with a relative you have been ignoring or feuding with; you can plan a regular lunch with a friend; you can start a book group that meets once a month; you can plan a regular card game or start some form of exercise with a friend you otherwise would hardly ever see; you can communicate with your elective representatives more than you do now; you can visit a museum you have been meaning to visit for years; you can attend your high school or college reunion; you can patronize a small local store or restaurant regularly and become friendly with the people who work there; you can say hello to toll takers; you can practice civility, even if others don't; you can go back to church or synagogue, or follow whatever your belief system dictates; you can eat family dinner as often as possible and read to your children whenever you can. These concrete steps, and others like them, can create a connected life for you. That will not only make you happier but make you live longer.[28]

In the context of our networks, a small win is making a small change in our daily routines that enables us to connect and bridge clumps. A small change can have a big benefit—as long as it's the *right* change. Small wins means we don't have to network *harder*, only *smarter*. Reflect on the three dimensions of networks described in Chapter Two: size, composition, and focus. Where should you seek small wins? The smart move is to adjust networks in a way that invokes the small-world effect. Unless your networks are very diverse already, seek empowering small wins by diversifying the composition of your networks and by externalizing their focus. Simply increasing the size of your networks won't do it. If you add someone who is just like you (or just like most people in your network), then your expanded network won't bridge clumps. Similar people have similar networks; they tend to live in the same clumps. Expanding networks to include dissimilar people is more likely to create the linchpin effect. Similarly, externalizing your focus to link up with new and diverse groups, associations, and organizations is more likely to create the linchpin effect than merely adding more of the same kinds of links. Composition and focus matter more than size.

There are two basic strategies for building entrepreneurial networks. The strategies are the same whether you work as a free agent (self-employed freelancer or independent contractor) or as a member of a large organization. In both contexts, the goal is to invoke the small-world effect by becoming a clump-bridging linchpin. Here are the two strategies:

1. *Build entrepreneurial networks by using preexisting programs, procedures, practices, organizations, and structures.* For example, if your company has a job rotation program, you can build clump-spanning networks by participating in the program.
2. *Build entrepreneurial networks by making new programs, procedures, practices, organizations, and structures.* For example, you can form your own "business forum" or "community of practice," providing a focus for people with common interests who are dispersed in various places.

The *application* of these strategies varies by context, so it's useful to discuss the challenges of building networks as a free agent and as an organizational member separately. Many of the examples work in both contexts, however, so you can benefit by studying both sections regardless of where you classify yourself. The purpose of the examples is to illustrate these strategies, give you ideas of what others have done, and stimulate your thinking. Even if you don't find a specific practice you can implement right away, think of how you could adapt or customize these practices to suit your particular needs and situation.

Building Entrepreneurial Networks as a Free Agent

Many sing the virtues of working solo: flexibility, setting your own hours, mastering your own fate; no more arbitrary bosses, no more inane corporate rules. Unlike those of their corporate peers, however, a free agent's networks don't come prepackaged and ready-made. In an organization, networks are created by the design of the organization itself. When I joined the University of Michigan Business School faculty, for example, I automatically had built-in opportunities for contacts: peer relationships (fellow members of the Department of Organizational Behavior and Human Resource Management), customer relationships (MBA students required to take the courses I taught), and support relationships (the departmental staffs of proficient secretaries, librarians, computer consultants, research assistants, and so on).

Free agents have to build their own opportunities for contact. My wife, Cheryl, was in this boat when we moved to Ann Arbor. As founder and president of HUMAX Corporation, she had built up her business in Chicago. Now in Ann Arbor, she had to start over again—finding new clients, getting venture capital, locating other free agents to subcontract with, finding suppliers, keeping up with new developments in her field, and so on. Her networks didn't come ready-made; she had to make them herself. It took time; it was a lot of hard work. But she and her business are thriving in Ann Arbor because she knows how to build empowering networks. (Later in this chapter, I will share with you some of the networking lessons she taught me.)

Strategy 1. Using preexisting programs,
procedures, practices, organizations, and structures
Even though a free agent's networks don't come ready-made, the environment does contain ready-made vehicles you can adopt as part of your network-building program. Remember the three

rules of real estate? Location, location, location. The same rules apply to building networks as a free agent: identify the places where people congregate, especially a mix of people. Diversity, as I've noted several times, means that the people you meet are likely to have non-overlapping networks, and that means connecting with linchpins, and *that* means invoking the small-world effect.

Sometimes the place is literally a *place,* a plot of real estate, that attracts diverse people with diverse networks. As *Business Week* writer Joan O'C. Hamilton discovered on her vacation, Hawaii is a place that attracts people who would be unlikely to meet elsewhere:

> As I sat beneath a swaying palm tree in Hawaii on my vacation, I heard a couple formulate, debate, and abandon an entire e-commerce business plan. It had something to do with printer drivers. And the whole episode took place in a single poolside sitting, punctuated only by his run for mai tais and her intervention in their toddler's tussle with another kid in the shallow end. But since most of the business planning took place in Geekspeak, I suspect the uninitiated within earshot were clueless.[29]

Who were these working vacationers? Hamilton had no idea, but I know—they were a fellow professor in my department, Anjali Sastry, and her husband, Mark O'Brien. Mark is chief scientist for Fineprint, a company that designs versatile printer drivers. Their favorite drink is the mai tai; their toddler son, Kiran, loves the pool.

Hamilton didn't have to introduce herself to Anjali and Mark for their networks to connect; sharing proximate space and time was enough. By overhearing and observing the family, Hamilton bridged her world and theirs. That's the first result of location in this story. Anjali told me about the *Business Week* story when we were discussing ideas for this book, and I had brought up the topic of location effects. How do I know Anjali?

We started our faculty jobs at the University of Michigan at the same time, and the Facilities Department put us in adjoining offices. Proximity meant that we had opportunities for countless impromptu conversations over the years. That's the second result of location. Now that we have new offices in separate buildings, we rarely bump into each other, and we talk only if we make explicit plans to meet. And that's the third result of location in this story. The three rules of real estate.

Some locations are better than others for making connections. Hawaii is a well-trodden crossroads in the world. Over five times as many tourists visit the islands as there are residents! Hawaii is a linchpinning place that helps to make the world's networks smaller. It improves the odds of unlikely events, such as my having this story to tell you.

Sometimes the place is not real but *virtual*—one of the new electronic meeting places such as bulletin boards and chat rooms. If you're not already tuned in to these virtual places, you might be skeptical of their potential. True, there is no substitute for the human moment of face-to-face interaction, but virtual meeting places have a significant role to play in helping build networks. Many expectant mothers, for example, don't tell others about their pregnancies until after the first trimester, in case something goes awry. The public bulletin boards sponsored by iVillage's "Parent Soup" offer a supportive world for pregnant mothers, as Jerry Davis and I documented in our case study.[30] The goal of the company is to "build a community of women on the Internet, and thereby to help them endure divorce, miscarriage, breast cancer, rude children, corporate stress, unfortunate taste in boyfriends, and whatever else a woman in the twenty-five-to-fifty-four demographic is likely to experience."[31] The Parent Soup site is enormous: it contains dozens of bulletin boards and tons of links about pregnancy, birth, child care, teens, family, marriage, divorce, relationships, education products, services, expert advice, fun and games, movies, religion, lifestyles, and so on. The bulletin boards for expectant mothers are organized by birth month (such as "Mothers of March 1999 Babies"). Our case study shows that they offer a positive environment for women to express their concerns and worries, support each other, and network on a wide variety of issues. For example, one mother we interviewed, a professional with advanced business degrees, was still a regular member of the electronic community ten months after giving birth to her second child. She typically logs on twice a day, a practice she started when she was just two months' pregnant. This electronic venue gave her opportunities to connect with a more diverse set of mothers than she would meet in her usual rounds of work and life:

I was really struck by the wide variety of people that were on the [bulletin] board in terms of their life circumstances. You would think that people that are on-line would be, you know, all highly educated and of a certain age, but there were all sorts of different circumstances. There were a lot of women who weren't married. There were a lot of women that were very young. There were some people that were having their first baby. There was one woman that was thirty-eight and having her sixth baby.

I am one of the oldest women on the board. There were plenty of women that were young enough to be my kid, easily. So it's a strange group. Well, I mean when you think about it, everybody just happened to be doing the same thing at the same time. It's the only real thing we have in common. If we had run across each other on the street we probably wouldn't necessarily be pals, but I mean, otherwise, what would I have in common with a lot of these women? But it's just not something you think about when you're on the board.

Her formal education, experience with her first birth, and business experience made her an important source of information for the community of mothers. She found herself offering advice on everything from child rearing to sources of medical information on the Web to personal and household finances. She lives in the Midwest but has become especially close with a lawyer from New York. They swap e-mail every day. The lawyer occasionally visits relatives in the Midwest, and the two are planning to meet face-to-face the next time the New Yorker is in the area.

The Hawaiian and virtual meeting places illustrate the same strategy: finding a preexisting place where a mix of people come together. You know that the world is organized around foci of common activities. The best network-building foci are those that attract a diversity of people.

Here are a number of practices that can actualize this strategy. Remember that you don't have to do everything; one or two wise choices may be all it takes to make your networks more entrepreneurial. Think about each practice and how you could use it to build your networks. Use Worksheet 3.1 to record your ideas on opportunities to implement each practice in your area.

#1. Live and work in Hawaii—or the networking equivalent. Of course, not everyone can live and work in Hawaii itself, nor would everyone want to. But you can elicit similar linchpinning effects if you live in the right building, neighborhood, or region. Most free agents have considerable latitude in picking their spots—where they live and where they work. Jeff Sanborn, a major in the U.S. Army, isn't exactly a free agent, but he used the latitude he had to make location work for him. When he returned to active duty after completing his MBA at the University of Michigan, he and his wife chose to live in on-base officers' housing, though they were permitted to have an apartment off-base. He learned from my course on networks and social capital that physical proximity would provide natural opportunities for chance encounters with fellow officers and would thus be the basis of building networks that spanned diverse army units.

Where are your customers, suppliers, and competitors? Where do they live; where do they work? You'll have to do some

■ Worksheet 3.1. Strategies and Practices for Free Agents ■

Strategy 1. Using preexisting programs, procedures, practices, organizations, and structures.

Practices	What opportunities are available in your area?
#1. Live and work in Hawaii— or the networking equivalent	
#2. Join a local business group	
#3. Teach a course	
#4. Join and become active in an association	
#5. Find a Web-enabled community	
#6. Volunteer for charitable activities	

Strategy 2. Making programs, procedures, practices, organizations, and structures.

Practices	What opportunities are available in your area?
#1. Invent your own "personal community."	
#2. Hitch your network to a linchpin's	
#3. Create a business forum	
#4. Found a Web-enabled community	

research to find the locations of highest density, but living and working in close proximity means you're likely to connect in an easy and natural way.

#2. *Join a local business group.* Business-oriented groups of all sorts abound in local communities. Their members are people like you, who are looking for ways to help others and improve their networks at the same time. The local chamber of commerce is a good place to start looking. Chambers often sponsor formal networking groups and events to enable their members to build networks and help each other. I've noticed a growing number of local entrepreneurial groups, from the informal to the formal. These are good examples of what to look for in your area. One is an informal group of young entrepreneurs who meet weekly at Dominick's restaurant, a popular business school hangout in Ann Arbor. The area also has the New Enterprise Forum (NEF), a nonprofit, all-volunteer organization "founded in 1986 to help area entrepreneurs grow their businesses by linking them with potential joint venture partners, mentors, business services, capital, and other critical resources." *U.S. News and World Report* calls NEF "the nation's most successful capital forum."[32] NEF's members include all sorts of entrepreneurs, marketing and management consultants, bankers, investors, lawyers, accountants, and so on. Another opportunity for free agents is the Ann Arbor IT Zone, founded in September 1999 by the local business community, the University of Michigan, and the city. The IT Zone's mission is "promoting the growth of our IT Industry by bringing together entrepreneurs, emerging and established companies, business service providers and university and community resources."[33] The IT Zone supports both an on-line and off-line IT community, business events, a Web site for networking, and a business assistance and conferencing center that incorporates the latest technology available. (For more details, you can visit the IT Zone's Web site at http://www.annarboritzone.org.) Your community probably has groups like these that you can join. Since they are always looking to grow, you can find them easily by scanning the events calendars in local newspapers or community Web sites.

#3. *Teach a course.* People from all walks of life take courses at local community colleges, community centers, university extension programs, and nonprofit organizations. By teaching a course you can make a solid contribution to the world while you broaden your networks. My editor, John Bergez, who works as a self-employed free agent, shared his experience after editing this chapter: "Speaking for myself, teaching editing courses in places like this for some years has resulted in a lot of the network benefits this chapter talks about. Even though I don't do it to 'get' (it would hardly be worth the investment!), former students are now important professional contacts, sources of work, etc. In some ways teaching seems like a perfect example of 'giving' via a network." I agree. If teaching a course sounds like too much, or seems too daunting, you can start with a small step. For example, you could volunteer to be a guest lecturer in someone else's course. Or you could give a free talk or lecture at a regular meeting of a nonprofit association, business group, or support group. These organizations are always looking for new speakers on interesting topics, especially those willing to give a talk for free.

#4. *Join and become active in an association.* There are plenty of opportunities to join associations, groups, and organizations. The sociometric survey in Chapter Two asked about your involvement in various types: professional associations, trade and industry associations, political parties, church or religious organizations, charitable or philanthropic organizations, art, music, or cultural organizations, self-help and personal development groups, and alumni groups. Some of these are local chapters of national or international organizations, such as the

Club of Rome (twenty-six associations worldwide) or the National Association for Female Executives (over two hundred networks in the United States, with others in the Netherlands, Israel, South Africa, and elsewhere). Consult the American Society of Association Executives for a comprehensive listing of thousands of local, state, and national associations and groups.

One of the best places to build entrepreneurial networks is the local chapter of your alumni association. First, alumni have a common bond; going to the same school, college, or university generates emotional bonds and lifelong connections. These common bonds provide a natural reason to come together. Second, alumni live and work in all sorts of places. Their networks don't overlap too much. An alumni association and its local chapters bridge these separate networks, providing a focal point to create powerful entrepreneurial networks. Join, attend, and volunteer to undertake some task or activity. For example, the University of Michigan Alumni NetWorks offers alumni the opportunity to request the services of a career counselor—or to become one. If you become a career counselor or informal mentor for alumni from your school, can you imagine the contributions you could make to others while you naturally built your networks?

Just joining an association and becoming active in it may be all it takes to build much more entrepreneurial networks. It's important, however, that you join one that you believe in. I am from the Chicago area, but I had moved away for quite a long time. When I returned to Chicago, a lot of people I knew had moved away. I was on the south side of the city at the University of Chicago and I didn't know many people. So I took my own medicine and said, "OK, what is it I like to do?" I like outdoor activities, hiking and mountaineering, that sort of thing, so I decided to join the Sierra Club. But the decision to join should not be solely for networking. If I had no interest in the Sierra Club—if I didn't support its mission and derived no pleasure from the outdoors—joining the organization to meet people would be a bad idea. Not only would I have little in common with the other members, people would wonder why I was there. It is important to join entities you believe in—associations, groups, and organizations that you feel passionate about.

#5. Find a Web-enabled community. Electronic communities solve the problem of small numbers: people who share interests or needs but are too widely scattered to create a community in a single physical place. There's not enough critical mass. For example, the chances are minuscule that enough pregnant mothers expecting in the same month would live in the same place to meet and form a workable community. Electronic communities allow isolated people to overcome the friction of distance and attain critical mass. As noted earlier, iVillage's "Parent Soup" birth-month bulletin boards allow women to contribute to others as they diversify their networks. Systers is an electronic community that serves a similar function for women in computer science. This forum was founded in 1987 by Anita Borg, currently president and founding director of the Institute for Women and Technology and a member of the technical staff at the Xerox Palo Alto Research Center, to overcome the constraints of gender imbalance in the computer field, where women are a small minority. It enables a critical mass of women in computer science to meet and interact. Systers now has over twenty-five hundred members in thirty-eight countries. (Visit their Web site for more information: http://www.systers.org.) Thus far, the world has seen only the beginning of the proliferation of Web-enabled communities. If you can't find one now that serves your interests, it's likely that it will appear in the future. Of course, you could found it yourself—but that's a topic for the next section.

#6. Volunteer for charitable activities. Doing charitable work, like teaching, is a great way to make a contribution to the world while you expand and diversify your networks. You're very likely to meet a diverse set of people from outside your usual circles—especially if you volunteer to do work in areas outside your usual professional interests. If you're not sure where to start, perusing local publications should give you plenty of names and places. You can also use the services of nonprofit organizations that help businesses and nonprofits link up. Business Volunteers Unlimited, for example, "serves businesses and nonprofits by promoting effective volunteerism and strengthening leadership." Among other services, the group places businesspeople on nonprofit boards. (For more information, see their Web site at http://www.businessvolunteers.org.) Age isn't a barrier. For example, Youth on Board helps young people to get involved in nonprofit organizations, often as actual board members. Their services include training, organizing, advocacy, and placement. The involvement of youth with nonprofits diversifies networks across the great intergenerational divide. (For more details, see the group's Web site at http://www.youthonboard.org.)

Strategy 2. Making programs, procedures, practices, organizations, and structures
It's often the case that a free agent can't find enough preexisting programs, procedures, organizations, or structures. The alternative is to invent them. Networks grow around a focus of common activities. You can use this "focusing effect" by creating new foci—venues of common activities.

Most people err by assuming that a network of like-minded individuals must exist before people can be mobilized around a common activity. The reverse is true: common activities breed a network of like-minded people. My colleague Bob Quinn offers this wise prescription for building a community: give people an instrumental task, hold them accountable, and a community will be born. The free agent's task, then, is to invent common activities to birth a network.

Here is a list of practices that can implement this strategy. This list is a little shorter than the one before, but don't let length fool you. Each practice described here is rich in opportunities. As before, use Worksheet 3.1 to record your ideas.

#1. Invent your own "personal community." A personal community is a network you construct around a specified mission, concept, or purpose. Personal communities are good for business; they are also good for the soul. Personal communities play an essential role in developing and expressing social identities, especially when you are in a major transition, such as graduating and taking a job, building a business, switching careers, returning to school, getting married, getting divorced, relocating, retiring, and so on.[34] Research on the use of these personal communities for successfully handling such transitions shows that entrepreneurial networks are usually better than closed networks.[35] Closed networks pen up people in old identities. Entrepreneurial networks enable people to explore new alternatives, experiment with different behaviors, build bridges to new worlds, and find new roles.

My wife, Cheryl, invented her own personal community after she and I moved from Chicago to Ann Arbor. As you read her story in the upcoming case study, you'll see that it contains all the elements for building networks that are good for business and good for the soul: a clear purpose, commitment, taking the first step, taking risks, moving outside of one's comfort zone, making contributions to others, being helped, trust, support, continuous evolution, and the vital interconnections of work, personal life, and the higher concerns of life. Cheryl's personal community today plays vital roles supporting her business, building her networks, and providing emotional support, friendship, and spiritual development.

Creating Personal Communities

My wife, Cheryl, and I made a joint decision to move from Chicago to Ann Arbor, where I had been offered a position to join the faculty of the University of Michigan Business School. We both recognized that I was moving into an organizational setting with ready-made opportunities for contacts, but that Cheryl would have to build her own personal communities. As the president and founder of HUMAX Corporation, she had built a thriving business in Chicago in the areas of personal and organizational development. She would have to rebuild in Ann Arbor.

She got started by meeting people in my department at formal events and informal occasions. "I would listen for the different connections of people who could support me," Cheryl recalls. "Bob was an example—a person that I could test the waters with. Or I would go out and have coffee with someone you recommended because you thought there would be a connection. Or someone in your community who is looking to support us, like Jane—she would recommend that I go talk with so-and-so. And I would go and talk to so-and-so."

"The pivotal moment was when I really made a commitment," Cheryl recalls, "when I saw that I had a unique contribution to make." This was the inception of what became her FutureSelf® Program for personal and professional development. "Once I made that decision, I started to see what kind of connections I wanted to create." A key person she met was Elizabeth, a seventy-two-year-old social worker, environmental activist, business consultant, and seminar leader. They met by accident, as so often happens in the world of networking. "It is such a funny story," Cheryl notes, "given that I was doing some copying for my business, standing in Kinko's, and I looked down and I saw somebody's brochure on some business that sounded rather interesting. The page that faced up was the person's picture, along with her bio. I started reading about how she described herself."

Two features of Elizabeth's brochure stood out for Cheryl. First, here was an older woman who was on her own. Second, she was very clear about her path. "Here is someone who has her own unique path," thought Cheryl, "and has implemented it. Here is someone who has done it." She asked for a copy of the brochure and called Elizabeth out of the blue. "I said, you don't know me, but I saw your brochure in Kinko's, and I like how you described yourself. Your business is very interesting to me and I would love to have a conversation and meet you." Their first meeting, scheduled for forty minutes, lasted more than three hours.

Cheryl and Elizabeth's budding relationship linked Cheryl to Elizabeth's set of relationships. "That connection connected me to a whole community that I would have never been connected to otherwise. She already had a premade community in Ann Arbor." Elizabeth proposed that Cheryl meet members of Elizabeth's personal community. "I was introduced to that community one by one. Nancy was the second person who joined us for monthly meetings. Basically, the original intention of our meetings was to support one another and build our businesses." Next, Lorna joined the group. She was a secretarial administrator, but was doing spiritual counseling on the side. She wanted to build up that side of the business.

Their meetings became opportunities for Elizabeth to reconnect with friends as she introduced them to Cheryl. "I sparked something," Cheryl says, "because these people had individual connections but were not meeting as a group. My introduction into their community reestablished their connection, and at the same time really built mine."

Over time, their original intention of meeting started to shift. "We started to recognize that whatever personal development issue was going on in our lives completely affected our business," recalls Cheryl. "Whatever we were learning about ourselves was somehow showing up in our business and is often what stops our businesses from moving forward. It became very intentional that our discussions were about both personal and business issues, and the connections between the two." Later, the purpose of the group evolved to include a spiritual component. "I can't describe it any other way," says Cheryl. "It was about our family, friendships, male-female companionship, and how all these aspects of our lives were interconnected. We started to call ourselves the Celestial Guardians. What really held the group together was our commitment to guard one another. We started to disclose really personal feelings, things that you certainly wouldn't tell your parents, and you may not even tell the people that are closest to you. I felt understood, I felt appreciated, I felt complete love and to this day I would say that it gave me the foundation to expand into areas that I was frightened of expanding into, work-related or not."

The Celestial Guardians continues to evolve. Recently, it considered merging with another group, where the combined groups could explore and develop their business, personal, and spiritual missions.

Cheryl's network continued to grow and expand, largely as a result of her active role in Ann Arbor. For example, she made a business connection with Roberta, someone she had met when Cheryl advertised her workshop at a local nonprofit business development center. She had been introduced to the center via the husband of one of my colleagues at the business school. When this colleague learned of Cheryl's new FutureSelf® Program, she asked her to run a workshop on it for the MBAs.

I should be clear that Cheryl didn't meet Roberta because Roberta *took* the center's workshop. The workshop had been cancelled due to lack of enrollment. Cheryl decided to offer free one-on-one FutureSelf® counseling to those who had signed up. Roberta took her up on the offer.

Roberta and Cheryl met several times after that counseling session to brainstorm about business. "One day Roberta happened to say, 'Oh by the way, I'm going to this workshop on Saturday about the Course in Miracles run by Unity Church and Marian Williamson.' I had heard about Marian Williamson from my friend Annette." They went together, and this experience gave birth to the creation of a spiritual group that includes people originally in Roberta's personal community, as well as some of Cheryl's friends.

In addition, Cheryl has taken regular courses at Landmark Education and Jerry Larkin's Doing Business the Zen Buddhist Way. These activities supplement her business knowledge and assist her personal development. They also help to make her networks more entrepreneurial. For example, she met and hired two consultants from these groups, people she would not have met in the normal round of life in Ann Arbor.

Source: Interview with Cheryl Baker. Used with permission.

#2. Hitch your network to a linchpin's. Every universe has linchpins like Kevin Bacon, Paul Erdös, Lois Weisberg, or Vernon Jordan. Hitching your network to a linchpin's network is like bolting on a turbocharger; it boosts your networking power by orders of magnitude. Who are the natural linchpins in the world

of free agents? They can be anywhere, but they're often found in professions and occupations that require networking for success, such as law, insurance, accounting, consulting, architecture, engineering, real estate, retail banking, and so on. For example, Cheryl was impressed with both the dentistry and the efficiently run office of our dentist, and so she asked him who his accountant was; his accountant is now the accountant for our personal affairs and for HUMAX Corporation. When Cheryl was looking for a lawyer for HUMAX, she asked our State Farm insurance agent; he recommended a lawyer in town, who is now HUMAX's attorney and our personal attorney.

#3. Create a business forum. If you can't find a business group, you can create one. The guidelines for building a business group are virtually the same as for building a personal community. You can create an informal group or a formal one. A business forum could be as simple as a monthly dinner you host at your home, inviting an assortment of people to attend. By doing so, you would help them build their networks as you built yours. At the formal end of the spectrum, consider the example of my acquaintance Robert Pasick, a clinical psychologist, personal leadership coach, business consultant, and author. In 1995, he conceived and founded The LEADership Forum—"a place for business leaders to meet in a safe, confidential setting with other leaders to discuss the challenges and stresses of being in charge."[36] Rob facilitates several forum groups, each of which meets once a month over dinner to discuss issues such as personal career development, balancing work and family, health, hiring and firing, strategic planning, and managing business relationships. Rob's principal intention is to help members of these groups by plying his psychological craft, but he also builds boundary-spanning entrepreneurial networks as he does so.

Don't neglect Web tools to help you run a business forum, informal or formal, especially the free Web services, such as Evite.com. Evite can help you coordinate and organize your activities and events. Evite sends invitations, tracks RSVPs, and automatically sends reminders. It provides details on your event, directions, and even a weather forecast. It lets guests post questions, and tallies and displays responses. (For access to free use of Evite, go to the Web site at http://www.evite.com.)

#4. Found a Web-enabled community. If you can't find a Web-enabled community, you can create one. This may sound like a daunting task, but it's easier today than ever before, and it will get easier as Web technology advances. It's not expensive, given the availability of free Web services, and you can start one from scratch. An example is the Vacuum Group, a network of about two hundred people scattered all over the globe but relatively concentrated in Ann Arbor and in California's Silicon Valley. Many members don't know each other outside of their participation in Vacuum. The group is devoted to understanding the intersection of "computer and people networks." Lately, the topic of the community has been network visualization tools.

Vacuum's founder Ed Vielmetti started the Web-enabled community when he was laid off from work, and he continued in earnest after he found a new job. I asked him to explain how he got the community off the ground and built its membership:

> I relied heavily on bootstrapping from other people who had existing similar network-based efforts (one fellow with a 3,000+ reader mailing list, another guy with a well-read weblog, a third with a regular dinner series) and then it sort of snowballed from there.
>
> There are a lot of ex–Ann Arbor people pretty much everywhere in the world, and the first round of contacts in a lot of situations are people who lived there once or went to school there.
>
> I'd say that perhaps 20 percent of the people on the mailing list found out about the group second or third hand. Word of mouth has also been how I've been included into other network events, where most of the time more like 80 percent of the

people are unfamiliar. I've gotten referrals to some pretty interesting people, who I don't think I'd ever have met otherwise.

For mailing list management, Ed used eGroups, a free, advertiser-supported service. (For details, visit the Web site at http://www.egroups.com.) For event planning, dinner outings, lunches, and so forth, he used Evite (the free service mentioned earlier in this chapter—see http://www.evite.com.) Vacuum's "weblog" (a "what's new" news clippings page) is maintained with Blogger (http://www.blogger.com).

To found a Web-enabled community, you should be clear on its purpose: What is its mission? What needs does it serve? Consider combining this practice with one of the others, such as building your personal community or business forum. Consider using the free Web services, such as those Ed used.

Building Entrepreneurial Networks as an Organizational Member

There's a widely perpetrated myth that the world is rapidly becoming a society of free agents—independent contractors, one-person consulting firms, and self-employed freelancers—and that anyone who doesn't become one has the brain power and career prospects of a dodo bird. Like most myths, this one contains some truth. But at the same time there's a trend in the *other* direction: the birth via megamerger of the biggest corporate leviathans ever to have swum the seas of business. There is more merger and acquisition activity now than ever before; in the United States alone, for example, the dollar value of merger and acquisition activity in 1998 exceeded $1.6 trillion.[37] Recent statistics from the U.S. Census show that most people still work in large organizations: almost half (48 percent) work in organizations with 500 or more employees; another 14 percent work in organizations with 100 to 499 employees; and another 18 percent work in organizations with 20 to 99 employees. Only 20 percent work in small organizations (those employing fewer than 20 people). Big organizations are here to stay, and building entrepreneurial networks in them will remain a perennial challenge.

I began the section on building free-agent networks by noting that organizations provide prepackaged, ready-made opportunities for contact. That's the good news. The bad news is that they also constrain networks. An organization is an "opportunity structure" that permits, encourages, and requires certain interactions; it is also a "constraint structure" that discourages, prohibits, and blocks other interactions. By design, every organization arranges joint activities along three dimensions: vertical, horizontal, and spatial. Vertical divisions define levels of authority and responsibility; horizontal divisions define common functions or tasks; spatial divisions define common locations of activity. Together, these create the foci of social networks in an organization. As sociologist Scott Feld observed, "Individuals whose activities are organized around the same focus will tend to become interpersonally tied and form a cluster."[38] These clusters (*clumps* in my terminology) make up the big world of an organization.

Unless you are mindful of the natural focusing effect of organizational design, your time, attention, and connections will be drawn inside a focused clump of organized activity, and your networks will become small and closed. Consider the story of a CFO of a well-known corporation, who took a social capital assessment (what he calls a "test" in the upcoming quote) during my social capital seminar, and realized—for the first time—that he had unwittingly allowed his networks to become too inwardly focused:

"It's too depressing."
"What's too depressing?" I asked.

"It's too depressing taking this test. It makes me realize what happened. All my connections were inside the finance department. I didn't know anyone outside the finance department, and I certainly don't know anyone outside the company. I've been downsized and out of work for two years, and now I know why I haven't been able to find another job. I don't have the network."

The illustrations in Figure 3.1 show stylized representations of three organizational contexts: start-ups, a multidivisional firm, and a university's student population. These are simplified for the sake of clarity. The real world, of course, is much more complicated, but its structure is the same—clumps of organized activity. As in any big world, linchpins provide the shortcuts that make it small. For the start-ups, the entrepreneurs and venture capitalists find each other through the social networks of friends, family, and business associates. In the multidivisional firm, entrepreneurial managers are the linchpins connecting levels, divisions, functions, and locations. And in the university setting, the bridges across cohorts of students are provided by clubs, fraternities and sororities, sports, and so on.

No matter which organizational setting you are in, the objective is the same: become a linchpin. There are more and less powerful ways of doing it. My colleague Jerry Davis offers this advice: "Start smoking." Now, of course he doesn't mean you have to take up this unhealthy habit. Rather, his remark illustrates the importance of identifying the places where a diverse set of people are likely to congregate. Where do smokers smoke? Rules force them to congregate in designated smoking areas, or outside near exits or in the alley. These areas are democratic; they draw people from all parts of the organization, people who normally would never encounter each other. Once they're back in the building, they return to their clumps.

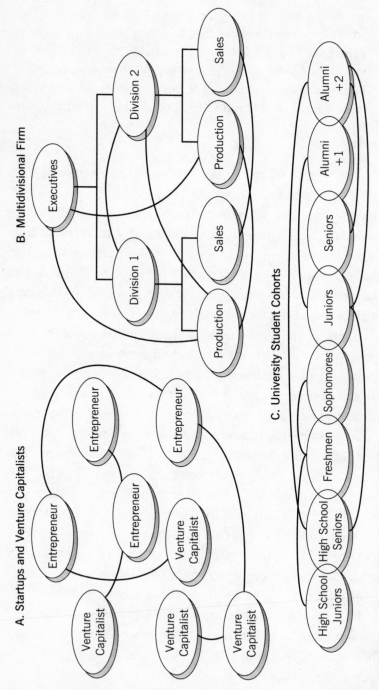

Figure 3.1. Three Simplified Illustrations of Clumpiness and Shortcuts

Strategy 1. Using preexisting programs,
procedures, practices, organizations, and structures

Entrepreneurial managers, says Harvard Business School professor Rosabeth Moss Kanter, reach beyond the boundaries of their formal positions to build ties and secure information, resources, and support.[39] No matter what your role is, any organization contains numerous opportunities to build entrepreneurial networks by using the design of the organization itself to reach outside of any given clump. Here are practices that work. Use Worksheet 3.2 to record your ideas about using these practices.

#1. Sit in the right place. The three rules of real estate—location, location, location—apply inside organizations as well as in a free agent's territory. There are natural crossroads inside organizations, just as Hawaii is a natural crossroads in the world's networks. Jeffrey Pfeffer tells a powerful story of a manager who attributes his success to his decision of where to sit:

> I know a man who was director of engineering for a division of Genrad Semiconductor Test Equipment, located in Milpitas, California. At the time, the division was housed in a typical California R&D building—open plan office, one level, and quite horizontally dispersed. His two predecessors had both been forced to resign, so it was clear that the position was a challenging one. The head of the division and his top managers had private offices along one wall of the building. After carefully studying the facility layouts, the new director of engineering decided not to occupy his office in the so-called Executive Row. He noted that during the course of the day, people walked to the cafeteria and to the washrooms. He found where the two paths tended to intersect, near the center of the open plan office layout, and took that position as his work location. He attributes much of his subsequent success to that simple move, since it gave him much better access to what was going on in his department. He could keep on top of projects, answer

■ Worksheet 3.2. ■
Strategies and Practices for Organizational Members

Strategy 1. Using preexisting programs, procedures, practices, organizations, and structures.

Practices	What opportunities are available in your organization?
#1. Sit in the right place	
#2. Find the dual roles	
#3. Rotate jobs	
#4. Join multifunctional committees, task forces, and teams	
#5. Volunteer for global assignments	
#6. Take advantage of educational and skills training opportunities	
#7. Externalize your networks	

Strategy 2. Making programs, procedures, practices, organizations, and structures.

Practices	What opportunities can you create inside or outside your organization?
#1. Mobilize a caucus group	
#2. Create a community of practice	
#3. Reach beyond the organization's walls	
#4. Think and act like a free agent	

informal questions, and in general, exercise much more influence over the activities of the unit than he could had he been off by himself.[40]

You may have more control over where you sit than you think you do. When you start a new job, for example, you may be given the opportunity to pick between various offices, cubicles, or desks. Or you might have the choice of which floor to be on. Even if you don't, you can request to be relocated when a vacancy opens up. Consider traffic patterns and identify the natural crossroads. You may also consider where others are sitting, and take a place in the vicinity of those whom you would like to meet. Proximity is a big determinant of interaction.

#2. Find the dual roles. A dual role is a formal position that spans two functions, departments, groups, units, teams, or locations. A dual role requires you to wear two hats. The production engineer is a classic example, where a single person bridges manufacturing and engineering, helping to coordinate their activities and mediate between the two. My acquaintance Roberta Zald holds a dual role as vice president of product engineering at Nematron Corporation in Ann Arbor. Nematron designs and builds hardware and software for industrial controls. Her dual role requires her to interface with product management, software development, and manufacturing. She also bridges to the outside through interactions with Nematron's contract manufacturers. Given her executive role in a medium-sized company, she also has significant interactions with the other parts of the organization, such as sales, marketing, accounting, purchasing, inventory, human resources, and service. As she put it, "This pretty much covers the entire organization chart."[41]

By design, dual roles create entrepreneurial networks. A dual role forces one to build ties across boundaries. Dual roles are natural network builders, but they can also subject their incumbents to role conflict and competing expectations, especially in traditional organizations designed around the normative principle of *unity of command*—the idea that each person should have only one boss.[42] Dual roles in traditional organizations are vaguely illegitimate. Today, however, dual roles abound in organizations, and multiple accountabilities are the rule and not the exception. We see, for example, the proliferation of dual roles such as co-chairs of committees, leaders of multiple teams, regional HR or finance managers, and so on. Even triple roles are possible. For example, my colleague Judy Olson holds a triple faculty appointment as a full professor in three different departments: Computer and Information Systems, Psychology, and Information and Library Services. What are the dual (or triple) roles in your organization? Do you qualify for them? If not, can you arrange your career to get the qualifications you need for them?

#3. Rotate jobs. Most organizations institute formal rotation programs, requiring employees to spend time working in different departments, functions, units, or locations. Some organizations restrict this practice to new hires; others mandate periodic rotations as part of a manager's ongoing career development. The Japanese are particularly deliberate about rotating managers and executives around the organization, giving them broad and varied business experiences. Building human capital—what you know—is one big purpose of rotation programs. Building social capital is another. Yet I've found that many people don't appreciate the enormous network-building power of job rotations. For example, I know a new general manager who spent three months rotating around different commercial storage facilities of a national storage and logistics company before taking charge of a new facility that was still under construction. He struggled to get his facility built and operational on time— but he failed miserably and was eventually fired. Why? It wasn't because he encountered novel problems without known solutions. His counterparts who ran other facilities had encountered and solved the same problems. They could have helped him. *But he never asked.* His rotations had given him the opportunity to

build a peer network spanning the various facilities. He could have kept in touch with his peers and asked them for advice when he needed it. But he saw the rotation program as a means to improve only his human capital, not his social capital. He didn't see that the company had handed him an easy and natural way to build entrepreneurial networks.

#4. Join multifunctional committees, task forces, and teams. Multifunctional groups naturally build entrepreneurial networks because, by their very design, they include members from diverse functions, disciplines, and levels. They are linchpinning devices. By participating in one, you'll diversify your network by meeting people from all over the organization. The effect will be just as if you had started smoking—but a lot healthier.

The supply of these network-building opportunities is rising: organizations are using multifunctional groups more today than ever before. But the demand is not. Many people consider serving on such groups to be a chore or a waste of time, and so they shun invitations to be on them. If you feel this way, consider the networking opportunities inherent in multifunctional assignments, not just the nature of their work. Of course, you should not accept a multifunctional assignment solely for networking purposes; making a meaningful contribution through the assignment is more important. But the contribution and networking potential should be considered together. For example, most universities are run by committees; my employer, the University of Michigan Business School, is no exception. We faculty make part of our contributions to the school by serving on various committees. It's expected. But our preferences are taken into account. When I was asked to run for election to the school's Strategic Planning Committee (SPC), I considered the committee's mission along with the network-building potential of the assignment. The SPC provides important inputs to the strategic direction of the school; its mission is reason enough to serve on it. But the network-building potential cinched it. By design, the

SPC includes members from different departments in the school. Two people from the same department never serve on it at the same time. Serving on the SPC means that one naturally meets faculty from other areas, often those whom one would not meet otherwise. For both reasons, I was glad to run for the committee, and pleased when I was elected.

#5. *Volunteer for global assignments.* As business globalizes, it's important that your networks do, too. Like job rotations or multifunctional groups, the purpose of global assignment is twofold: It builds your human capital by broadening your cultural and business knowledge while it globalizes your networks. And just as with job rotations or multifunctional groups, I've found that many people underrate the importance of the second purpose: building entrepreneurial networks. For example, my former employer, the University of Chicago Graduate School of Business, started an international Executive MBA program in the early 1990s. The teaching facility was located in Barcelona, Spain, but attracted students from around the globe. Many colleagues declined to teach in the program because it seemed like more work (it was necessary to revamp courses to include more international content) for the same pay (we didn't get paid extra). I had previously evaluated my networks, using an instrument like the one you used in Chapter Two, and concluded that my networks were much too domestic for a professor of business. So I jumped at the offer to teach in Barcelona, knowing that the experience would provide opportunities to globalize my networks. I won't bore you with all the details, but it worked out even better than I hoped. For example, my first book, *Networking Smart*, was translated into Spanish and republished in Barcelona; I returned and gave a talk in the Madrid Chamber of Commerce; I returned again and gave a workshop on networks and social capital at IESE, a leading Spanish business school. My first trip to Spain was the origin of all these experiences.

Experts predict a rising trend in the number and type of opportunities for global work—short-term or long-term assignments abroad, working for a foreign subsidiary in your home country, working on cross-national teams, and negotiating with representatives from foreign companies.[43] The globalization of work is inevitable. You can stay ahead of this trend—and improve your ability to contribute to your company, colleagues, and customers—by globalizing your networks as well.

#6. Take advantage of educational and skills training opportunities. Most companies offer a variety of training opportunities, ranging from short workshops to long-term degree programs. Some companies, like Xerox, American Express, and Wells Fargo, even offer personal growth and social service leaves for volunteer charitable work. These mini-sabbaticals vary from a few weeks to a year, and sometimes include pay and benefits.

Like the practices I've discussed so far, the purpose of educational and skills training programs is to build human capital and social capital at the same time. Content and need should be the main reasons for taking a program, but always consider network-building potential in the process. These programs are natural venues for building entrepreneurial networks. In-house programs provide chances to meet and interact with peers from around the company, often those you wouldn't meet otherwise. These programs enable you to build connections that span the organization's internal boundaries. External programs provide opportunities to diversify your networks outside the company. Usually, a mix of in-house and external programs is better than just one or the other. One company I know, for example, mandates regular educational programs for its executives and managers, but restricts them to internal programs. The company culture discourages its executives and managers from getting involved with outside associations, groups, or organizations. As a result, their networks have narrowed over time, and now are much too inwardly focused, especially for the leaders of a large organization. Regular doses of external programs would help to reverse the problem.

#7. Externalize your networks. The typical organization is enmeshed in an external network of customers, suppliers, investors, joint ventures, strategic alliances, and so on. This external network provides ready-made opportunities to externalize your networks. For example, an engineer I know volunteered to serve on his company's alliance management committee. The committee was formed to provide a single point of coordination for the company's growing network of alliances. His job on the committee required him to travel regularly to visit with the company's alliance partners, understand their strengths, capabilities, and needs, and seek ways to pool resources, link systems, or jointly exploit market opportunities. His networks became more entrepreneurial as a natural by-product of doing his committee work. He became the linchpin in his company's external network of alliances, bridging clumps of disparate and diverse organizations. Not only was he more effective at managing each individual alliance relationship, he also saw opportunities to introduce and link together two or more alliance partners, closing the structural hole between the partners themselves. Indeed, he proposed an "alliance fest" in which all the company's alliance partners could come, meet each other, and explore ways to ally with each other.

Explore similar opportunities in your own organization: committees, task forces, or teams overseeing customer relations, supplier partnerships, or strategic alliances. Can you join one of them? Other options include volunteering to work in a joint venture—or simply spending more time at customers' sites or visiting suppliers on their home turf. For example, when Bob Cantwell was CEO of Hadady Corporation, a parts supplier to companies such as Caterpillar, he arranged personal contacts between his people and his suppliers.[44] If he had a quality problem with a Hadady product, Bob would send the Hadady machine operator along with the customer service representative to the customer's site. This networking practice not only led to better solutions, it also externalized people's networks.

Strategy 2. Making programs, procedures,
practices, organizations, and structures
Organization design boxes us in. All designs, but especially traditional ones, constrain the formation of entrepreneurial networks, discouraging, prohibiting, or blocking ties that cross organizational boundaries. If your organization doesn't provide the prepackaged, ready-made opportunities for contact that you need, then you can make your own opportunities. There are ways to work in, through, around, parallel to, or against the design of an organization. This isn't as difficult as it may appear, because contemporary organizations are no longer the static and stable structures they once were. Today's organizations undergo endless rounds of change, restructuring, and transformation. Frequent organizational change creates the space to make your own programs, procedures, practices, organizations, and structures.

#1. Mobilize a caucus group. A caucus group is a grassroots organization of employees who band together to overcome organizational barriers. These barriers can be formal, such as hiring and promotion policies, or informal, such as a culture that permits discriminatory practices. For example, black professionals hired by Xerox in the 1970s were given poor sales territories as a result of racial discrimination in the assignment of people to territories.[45] An informal system of matching internal job candidates and job openings blocked their opportunities for advancement. The black professionals were excluded from Xerox's informal networks, so they rarely found out about openings until after they were filled.

Black professionals responded by mobilizing caucus groups. The first was BABE, for Bay Area Black Employees, in San

Francisco. Others arose spontaneously in New York, Washington, D.C., Chicago, and elsewhere. Each caucus group was self-funded, and members met on their own time, giving each other advice, training, moral support, mentoring, and information. They lobbied successfully for changes in Xerox's hiring and promotion policies. The members of each caucus group came from different levels and locations in Xerox, making the caucus group a natural venue for building boundary-spanning entrepreneurial networks. The leaders of the various caucus groups developed their own network, making the big world of Xerox smaller by linking distant groups. And in the course of fighting for organizational change, they met and built ties with top executives at Xerox. The Xerox black caucus groups were so successful at advancing their cause while effecting organizational improvements that they are now widely imitated by other groups, such as Hispanics, Asians, and women, and have become a role model of "best practices" in human resources by companies such as GE.

Caucus groups come in all shapes and sizes. A few years ago, women professors at the University of Michigan Business School founded Neighbors, an informal network that cuts across departmental lines and faculty ranks. The reason was simple, as Jane Dutton, a founding member, explains: "Women didn't know other women at the school. We wanted to meet to get to know each other in a manner that helped our careers." Departments are classic examples of clumps, and faculty women were scattered across departments, sometimes just one per clump. Clumps confine networks, and so the women had few natural venues in which to meet.

Like the people in the black caucus groups, members of Neighbors decided to fund their own activities and meet on their own time. The group convenes once a term for a dinner meeting, hosted at a different faculty member's home each time. Dinner is potluck. Each meeting is devoted to a specific topic, such as teaching in the school's Executive Education programs, sharing research, women's health and exercise, and so on. Participating in Neighbors helped everyone, from newcomers who felt welcomed to senior professors who had been isolated in departments and now felt a strengthened sense of attachment to the school. And, like the caucus groups, Neighbors produced positive changes for everyone, not just its members. For example, during a discussion of teaching, a perennial problem came up: When the professor teaching in the class period before yours is running over, how do you get the person to pack up and move out? This problem was presented to the deans, who issued a memo to all faculty, requesting each teacher to respect the needs of the next, and to be sure to exit the classroom at the scheduled time. Dual-career couples was another problem identified and solved. Neighbors learned that three junior faculty members were considering leaving because their partners were not living in the area. Neighbors raised this problem with the deans, resulting in new policies and practices that help both men and women, such as hiring a headhunter to work with spouses, male or female, and systematically tapping the alumni network.

#2. Create a community of practice. A community of practice is a formal or informal network of people who work in the same function or process but are geographically distributed. Geographic separation creates clumps that must be bridged by networks to create a community of practice. For example, the powertrain engineers of a global auto maker, who work in units (clumps) around the world, have the makings of a community of practice. They work on similar powertrain problems, and could save time and money by sharing knowledge—a problem in one clump may well have been solved already in another, and if the engineers had a way to network across clumps, they could link up the problem and its solution. To function as a community, therefore, potential members must have a mechanism for

communicating, linking problems and solutions, sharing and storing knowledge, and organizational learning.[46]

The original communities of practice were informal, grass-roots networks of frustrated repair technicians who banded together to solve common problems.[47] Today, however, the concept of communities of practice is widely imitated, and you see them in all functional and process areas of an organization. All sorts of media are used, including the telephone, fax, e-mail, video conferencing, face-to-face meetings, electronic bulletin boards and newsgroups, group decision support systems, computer-aided systems, and more. Some firms, such as Ford Motor Company, have institutionalized the concept, allocating company resources to encourage and support communities of practice. Agile organizations promote organizational learning by linking multiple communities of practice.[48] However, you don't have to wait for or depend on organizational support. Like the founders of the original communities of practice, you can create your own, recruiting via the snowball method—asking the counterparts you know in other units, getting them to recruit people they know, and so forth. Web resources such as eGroups (http://www.egroups.com) provide free or inexpensive networking technologies. Communityware tools such as I-KNOW, created and developed in the Team Engineering Collaboratory at the University of Illinois, offer easy-to-use electronic technologies for a far-flung network of people to stay in contact, communicate, and share information.[49]

#3. Reach beyond the organization's walls. One of the great dangers of working inside an organization is that networks tend to stop short at its boundaries. The nature of some jobs, like sales or purchasing or investor relations, forces people to build ties beyond the organization's walls. Most people's networks, however, are internally focused. To combat this tendency, it's important that you deliberately reach beyond the organization's walls. If you can't externalize your networks by tapping into

preexisting relationships with customers, suppliers, or alliance partners, then you have to build your own external links. You have several options. The simplest is to join an existing association in your area of specialty; no matter what your functional expertise may be, there is an association that serves it. These types of associations help you diversify your networks across companies and industries, but they still confine your networks within your particular specialty. Another option, therefore, is to join an existing association that serves members of diverse disciplines as well as diverse companies and industries. For example, in Chapter Two I described Tom Caprel's involvement in TEC, the seven-thousand-member worldwide organization for executives and managers of companies ranging from small entrepreneurial firms to big corporations.

If you can't find an existing group, create one. For example, years ago women working as investment bankers on Wall Street were denied membership in the Investment Association of New York, a venerable but all-male organization of investment bankers. So they banded together and founded the Young Women's Investment Association, now named the Financial Women's Association (FWA) of New York. FWA thrives today, with more than a thousand members, more than a hundred corporate sponsors, and an impressive financial endowment.[50] Similarly, women in the new media got together and created Webgrrls, a 750-member networking group in the New York area. Other examples include Advertising Women of New York, the Committee of 200, and Women Rainmakers (an offshoot of the American Bar Foundation). Yet another example is the peer mentoring network created by the academic chairs of management and organizational behavior departments in six different business schools.[51] Traditionally, department chairs work in isolation, without mentoring or even much contact with other chairs. Yet they encounter the same problems. With the guidance of an expert in mentoring, Kathy Kram, then department chair at

Boston University, the six formed a peer mentoring project. They met three times a year as a group and held group conference calls once a month, with informal contacts and calls in between. This peer network helped the chairs with a host of common problems, such as course scheduling, issues of equity in regard to teaching load, and performance reviews and pay concerns.

#4. Think and act like a free agent. Like it or not, for better or for worse, this is the age of free agency even for organizational members. The days of lifelong employment are over. Staying for a long time in one job or in one company is no longer a badge of honor. In fact, it raises eyebrows—and suspicions—about a person's abilities and ambition. Bret Chennault discovered this stigma after working for a major automobile manufacturer for fifteen years. An engineer by training, Bret worked in a combination of sales, marketing, and training. "When my counterparts [at other companies] find out that I've been with one company for fifteen years, they're shocked. For me, I thought that was a benefit, not a problem. That was one of the things I needed to overcome—being with one company for fifteen years." Prospective employers feared that a decade and a half with one firm might have turned Bret into a conservative, old-school manager. "I needed to offset that with something. First impressions mean a lot. I thought about what would project an image of myself as a person who is forward thinking, up to speed with technology, and so forth. The Palm Pilot attracted my attention." Bret used his Palm Pilot during interviews to record notes, jot down phone numbers, enter dates and times of events, and so forth. In addition to the practical utility of a Palm Pilot, using it produced the desired impression. "I can tell you that three out of five times that I used it, pulling it out immediately resulted in some sort of positive comment. 'How do you like that?' 'Oh, you got one of those?' 'Isn't that one of those Day Timers?' This allowed me to go into the details of what it can do. And it supports that image

that this guy is up to date on everything." Bret now is senior project manager with Urban Science Applications, Inc., a leading information and marketing supplier to the automotive and other industries around the globe.

A highlight of Bret's story is the use of technology; in his case, a Palm Pilot. I am a fan of technology because it helps good networkers keep track of the people they know, so they can bridge structural holes quickly and efficiently. There's nothing much worse than losing the contact information of someone you would like to help! Personally, I use four devices: Palm Pilot, ACT! (a contact manager), Eudora e-mail, and customized Web pages. I dabble with Evite and eGroups, both of which I described earlier. Technology is a tool; it's not an end in itself. It doesn't matter if you keep drawers full of paper files and rubber-banded stacks of business cards or you digitize every scrap of information and become completely paperless. What works for you works. The goal is to stay organized.

But the larger point of Bret's story is the need to think and act like a free agent even when you're working as a member of an organization. Consider all the practices I advised for free agents—joining or creating a local business group, teaching a course, finding or founding a Web-enabled community, inventing your own personal community, hitching your network to a linchpin's, and so on—and think about how you could adapt these practices for building entrepreneurial networks inside and outside your organization.

■

The preceding sections provide dozens of suggestions and examples for making your networks more entrepreneurial. These practices work. But they are mere words on paper until you act. You now know *what* to do. You have to couple *what* to do with the *will* to do. Only you can change your behavior.

■ The Will to Change

Using any of these suggestions requires a change of behavior on your part. There's no way around it. To implement a practice you have to move out of your comfort zone, change your daily routines, and step outside the normal rounds of your life. Change requires a will to change. After coaching many people over the years, I've learned a few lessons that might help.

• *Discomfort is good.* Most people interpret discomfort as a warning sign telling them to avoid something. The opposite is true for networking. Discomfort is a sign that you're doing something *right.* If you're not feeling uncomfortable, then you aren't moving out of your comfort zone. For example, meeting someone who is just like you is more comfortable than meeting someone who is different from you, but meeting dissimilar people diversifies networks. So if you feel discomfort, forge ahead— you're doing the right thing. As with any skill, the more you do it, the better you'll become and the more comfortable you'll feel.

• *Behavior first, attitude later.* Many people wait until they have prepared the right internal state of mind before they change their behavior. For example, they want to feel confident before they act confidently. These people never change. They don't because they have cause and effect backwards. New attitudes don't precede new behaviors; the reverse is true—new behaviors create new attitudes. Act confidently, and you become confident. Psychologists call this the *as if* principle. Act as if you are something and you become that something. Applied to networks, the as-if principle prescribes that you should stride forth and build networks; only then will you develop the attitude of a network builder.

• *See network opportunities.* Once, as a guest on WGN talk radio in Chicago, I had a caller who said, "I work sixty to seventy hours a week and I have no time to do any networking!" Lack of time is a common complaint. My response was that you are surrounded by network-building opportunities. But you see them only if you look for them. Evaluate all the opportunities that come your way. Make it a natural part of the work you do, a natural part of your life. Ask that one additional question, What is the networking potential in this opportunity?

- *Seek small wins.* In this chapter I've mentioned my colleague Karl Weick's concept of "small wins" as the embodiment of wisdom. It's worth mentioning again. Small steps can yield big payoffs. You have to do only a few small things to achieve big improvements in building your networks. Review your responses on Worksheets 3.1 and 3.2. Which practice would make your networks more entrepreneurial *and* be easy for you to do? Start with that one.

- *Make a contract.* Good intentions don't lead to action; commitments do. Make a contract with yourself to take the step you picked for your first small win. Be specific—who, what, when, where—and write it all down. A written contract feels more binding than an oral contact. Even better, find a partner and exchange written contracts. Hold each other accountable; support each other; report your progress and check on your partner's. Make a public commitment: announce your contract to close friends, your family, or another trusted group. Ask for their support; ask them to hold you accountable; ask them to check on your progress.

CHAPTER SUMMARY

The overarching lesson of this chapter is to be the architect of your personal and business networks, consciously and deliberately building networks that enable you to achieve your goals, fulfill your mission, and make your contribution to the world. For most people, the objective is to build networks that are more entrepreneurial—larger, more diverse, more outwardly focused—than the networks they have now. Before attempting to change existing networks, however, it is necessary to grapple with the "for what" question: What do you use social capital for?

For many, the answer is what they can get from their networks—information, advice, leads, sales, jobs, financial capital, emotional support, and so on. However, a focus on getting isn't a powerful or empowering reason for building networks. Service to others—giving—is the best reason for building better networks. Helping others helps you. Paradoxically, you are helped in proportion to how little you focus on what you get and how much you focus on what you give. Of course, focusing on what you can get from others does work—but only in the short run. Whether you view it as a moral mandate or simple pragmatics, the prescription for long-term success is to build better networks so that you can use them to contribute to others.

Building better networks relies on a universal law: the *small-world principle.* Understanding this principle provides deep insights into the way in which the world is organized and why entrepreneurial networks are so effective. It turns out that the world is *clumpy*—that is, organized into regions of densely interconnected people and organizations. Most people live in clumps, and their networks are confined inside them. However, the presence of a few shortcuts across the clumps creates the small-world effect. The shortcuts are created by *linchpins*—people who know members of many diverse clumps and can provide bridges between them. It is possible to maximize the small-world effect by becoming a linchpin, building entrepreneurial networks that span diverse and disparate clumps. The more you invoke the small-world effect, the closer you put yourself to all the resources you need.

This chapter delved deeply into what you can do: proven practices to make your networks more entrepreneurial. It considered two strategies in two contexts, as a free agent and as an organizational member. The first strategy recommends using preexisting programs, procedures, practices, organizations, and structures; the second calls for making new programs, procedures, practices, organizations, and structures.

Of course, all the theory, advice, and examples packed in this chapter amount to nothing unless you take action. Only you can do that. But if you do, you will build powerful and empowering networks that you can use to achieve your goals, fulfill your mission, and make your contributions to the world. Using the networks you've built is the topic of the next chapter.

Using Your
Social Capital

magine yourself in this situation. You're a national account representative for the Acme Company, working hard to establish yourself as the company's top salesperson. Acme recently hired you away from Vertex Corporation, a major competitor, where you were a rising star. At Acme, you've been building a relationship with a new customer, one you haven't done business with before, but you feel you're on the verge of closing a major deal. However, you learn that this customer's needs would be better met by purchasing a similar product from Vertex. Acme's product would meet the customer's technical specifications. What would you do? Would you go ahead and close the sale, or would you introduce the customer to your contacts at Vertex? Think about it, and indicate your answer here:

Check one:

❑ I would sell the Acme product to the new customer.
❑ I would introduce the customer to Vertex.

This small scenario illustrates how the pattern of connections and disconnections in a network is an opportunity structure (see Figure 4.1). Someone who stands in the gap or structural hole between disconnected people, groups, or organizations enjoys an advantage. In this scenario, the advantage is superior knowledge: You know about the customer's needs but your former employer doesn't; the new customer knows about your product but not your former employer's. The crux is what to do with this opportunity structure. Do you maintain the gap between alters, or do you close it?[1] The "union" strategy loses a sale but creates immediate value for the customer and your former employer; as a result, you garner gratitude and appreciation. The "disunion" strategy yields an immediate sale, but you're left knowing that it's not in the customer's best interest.

This scenario represents the ethical dilemma at the heart of social capital: How do we use it? The mere thought of "using"

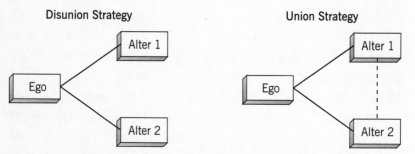

Figure 4.1. **Illustration of Network Dilemma**
Source: Adapted from Wayne E. Baker and David Obstfeld, "Social Capital by Design: Structures, Strategies, and Institutional Context," in Roger Th. A. J. Leenders and Shaul M. Gabbay (eds.) *Corporate Social Capital Liability* (Norwell, Mass.: Kluwer, 1999), chapter 4, figure 1. Used by permission.

social capital conjures up more negative images than positive ones. The American language contains many synonyms for the negative connotations of *using:* exploiting, manipulating, taking advantage of, using for one's own ends, working or playing upon, imposing on, milking, bleeding, and so on. Someone who uses people is a "user" or an "opportunist." Yet no one can avoid deciding how to use social capital. In the Acme-Vertex scenario, suppressing useful information is as much a decision as choosing to share it. As in most situations in life, doing nothing is as much a choice as doing something. The question, therefore, is not *whether* to use social capital but *how* to use it.

This chapter explores why the better alternative in the opening scenario is to close the gap and give up the sale. This may sound naive, Pollyannaish, or even irrational. But there are sound scientific as well as ethical reasons for using the union strategy. The most successful networkers adopt the viewpoint discussed in Chapter Three: the purpose of building networks is to contribute to others. From this perspective, using social capital means putting networks into action in service to others. Why is this alternative superior in the long run? Because it invokes one of the most powerful principles in human life: *reciprocity.* Reciprocity is the engine of networks. We are helped because we help others. When we harness the power of reciprocity, our social capital multiplies, like a good investment. By contrast, construing reciprocity narrowly—"You scratch my back, and I'll scratch yours"—can work in the short term, but it's self-limiting.

■ The Power of Reciprocity

On September 19 and 20, 1985, devastating earthquakes wracked Mexico City. The main quake measured 8.1 on the Richter scale; its aftershock was 7.5, bigger than most earthquakes. Over twenty thousand people died, and a hundred thousand were left homeless. International relief agencies rushed aid from around the world to the victims. Among the contributors was the Ethiopian Red Cross, which donated $5,000. This amount may not seem large, but Ethiopia is one of the poorest nations on earth. Hundreds of thousands of its citizens have died from starvation brought on by extensive famines, and $5,000 would have fed many Ethiopians. Why did Ethiopia send money to Mexico City? Psychologist Robert Cialdini explains that it was "because Mexico had sent aid to Ethiopia in 1935, when it was invaded by Italy. . . . The need to reciprocate had transcended great cultural differences, long distances, acute famine, and immediate self-interest."[2] In this instance, the impulse to reciprocate was powerful enough to overcome the donor's pressing needs, not to mention the passage of more than sixty years.

Reciprocity also explains the aid Australia gave to East Timor. The East Timorese suffered for years at the hands of the Indonesians; in 1999, their vote for independence prompted a bloody invasion and mass deportations. The Australians decided to help because of help they had received fifty years earlier. Among the strongest supporters of Australia's effort were retired servicemen who remember the aid the East Timorese gave them during World War II, for which the East Timorese were severely punished by Japan. By the same token, the *lack* of reciprocity explains the troubled relations between the United States and France after World War II, as Wilton Dillon explains in *Gifts and Nations*.[3] Proud France was doubly humiliated, first by its defeat by Nazi Germany and second by its rescue and reconstruction by Allied powers, especially the Americans. America's inability to define ways in which France could repay American aid—that is, reciprocate—instigated years of political discord and enmity between countries that had been friends since the American Revolution. (Indeed, the French refer to Americans as their "old friends.")

If reciprocity is a powerful principle in the world of international relations—where narrow self-interest often seems to be king—can it be any less powerful in everyday life? Consider a business case of the power of reciprocity, which concerns an acquaintance of Robert Cialdini's:

> She sells radio advertising time on the station she works for to a large range of clients. My friend has the reputation of being the best radio advertising salesperson in the city. She's frequently being offered attractive positions at rival radio stations and is always rising to the top of the sales staff at whichever station employs her.
>
> Because she has clients in a variety of businesses, she is always on the lookout for any business leads that she can pass on to them. If, for example, she learns through her contacts in the food industry that a new supermarket chain is thinking of moving into town, she instantly calls all of her clients who could profit from that information: the construction companies, the Realtors, the banks, the advertising firms—any of her customers who could send out salespeople to try to get the new supermarket chain's business before their competitors do.
>
> She reports that the gratitude that she gets is immediate, and that the obligation her clients feel to her is long term, especially among those who actually land the chain's account. They do everything they can to return the favor by giving her all their business that they can possibly justify. The same sort of reciprocal arrangements apply virtually everywhere.[4]

Here's one more example of reciprocity, this one from the inner workings of a corporate giant. British Petroleum (BP) fosters learning across business units by instilling the principle of reciprocity. BP doesn't use the label "reciprocity," but you'll recognize the principle in practices such as "peer assists" and "personnel transfers." As Jeffery Pfeffer and Robert Sutton describe, these practices involve one BP business unit's lending its talented people to work in another business unit.[5] BP's incentive system should prevent such practices, because the company measures and rewards performance at the business unit level. Pfeffer and Sutton note that the lending unit loses the talents of people "on loan" and does not get any measurable credit for the borrowing unit's success. Yet business unit managers willingly and frequently share their people with each other. Why? Reciprocity. Managers know that they will need help in the future. A manager who loans staff to another unit can rightly expect reciprocation in the future. In the long run, the units themselves and the company as a whole benefit from reciprocal exchanges of personnel across business unit boundaries.

You could probably think of many similar stories. The reciprocity principle works because it is universal; sociologist Alvin Gouldner calls it one of the "principal components" of all moral codes.[6] The principle governs all human relations, from the international to the interpersonal, from aboriginal to postindustrial societies.[7] Indeed, the principle is so fundamental that it has been said to *define* humanity: "We are human," says archaeologist Richard Leakey, "because our ancestors learned to share their food and their skills in an honored network of obligation."[8] Charles Darwin makes a similar remark in *The Descent of Man*.[9] Sociologist Howard S. Becker argues that we should call ourselves "*Homo reciprocus*" (man who reciprocates) instead of "*Homo sapiens*" (man the wise).[10] The principle of reciprocity explains why building social capital works: When you use your networks to contribute to others, others contribute to you. Series of reciprocal acts build what French anthropologist Marcel Mauss called systems of "well-balanced chains of reciprocal services."[11] The uniquely human "network of obligation" or "web of indebtedness"[12] laid the groundwork for trade, the division of labor, and complex social organization. "For the first time in evolutionary history," Cialdini summarizes, "one individual could give away any of a variety of resources without actually giving them away. The result was the lowering of the natural inhibitions against transactions that must be *begun* by one person's providing personal resources to another. Sophisticated and coordinated systems of aid, gift giving, defense, and trade became possible, bringing immense benefit to the societies that possessed them."[13]

In contrast, unethical practices throw the system out of balance. Cialdini warns that the rule of reciprocity is so overpowering that it enforces uninvited debts and triggers unfair exchanges.[14] A host of psychological and sociological experiments documents the force of reciprocity in human relationships: a person's deeply felt obligation to repay a benefit received from another.[15] Failure to repay violates human psychological makeup and cultural conditioning. But these experiments show that even the act of giving something *unwanted* or *unasked for* invokes the need to repay. And so the rule of reciprocity can be unfairly invoked in order to manipulate others. Cialdini describes several unethical practices.[16] For example, members of the Hare Krishna sect obtain monetary contributions by employing the *donation-request* tactic. By giving the target a "gift"—a religious book, a flower, or a small American flag—they create an uncomfortable "debt" that the target discharges by giving cash in return. Many nonprofit organizations use this tactic in direct mail campaigns, sending targets unsolicited gifts of greeting cards, colorful stamps, calendars, and the like. Similarly, marketers give free samples to induce feelings of indebtedness relieved by making purchases.

Another example of a manipulative use of reciprocity is the *rejection-then-retreat* tactic, which yields compliance by creating a false concession.[17] Suppose someone makes an unreasonable request of you. When you reject it, the person counters with a smaller request. This planned retreat to a smaller request appears as a concession, which you feel indebted to reciprocate by making a concession in return—acceding to the smaller request. This is a favorite ploy of door-to-door salespeople. For example, a salesperson who counters your rejection of a product with a request for referrals (names of your friends or neighbors) employs a version of the rejection-then-retreat tactic.

Even ethical practices can impede genuine reciprocity. The common "transactional" orientation thwarts the power of reciprocity. Many people conceive of their business dealings as spot market exchanges—value given for value received, period. Nothing more, nothing less.

This tit-for-tat mode of operation can produce success, but it doesn't invoke the power of reciprocity and so fails to yield extraordinary success. For example, some business schools (not Michigan) preach and practice an extreme market philosophy. These schools treat students like transactions—education given for tuition received. Alumni often express their reactions this way: "I got my money's worth—and not a cent more. I don't feel any obligation to the school." It seems as if they *want* to feel obligated—to *belong*—but feel the school treated them like a cold transaction. It's no surprise that these schools suffer from weak alumni networks and poor records of alumni donations. Alumni who don't feel obligated to their schools rebuff pleas to "give something back." Schools that preach a severe market philosophy reap what they sow.

A variation of the transactional mode of operation is what I call "coin-operated networking." Not so long ago, I was invited to give a talk on social capital to an audience of financial advisers. Or rather, they called themselves "advisers"—but really they were salespeople. Their bosses wanted me to address the group because they knew that "networking" (as they termed it) was an essential "sales skill" (also their term). As the time approached for my talk, I walked through the hotel lobby toward the conference room, encountering along the way one of the financial advisers. I introduced myself and asked about her expectations for the seminar. "Our problem is that we want immediate results," she said. "We don't want to spend a lot of time 'networking.' When I spend fifteen minutes with someone, I expect their business. When I don't get it, I say, hey, this 'networking' is a waste of time. I want instant results." She was talking about coin-operated networking: a mechanical view of human relationships where a deposit of a few minutes is expected to get immediate results every time, as the drop of a coin in a gumball machine always produces a gumball. Her attitude conveyed all the nuances of a tit-for-tat understanding of reciprocity: a one-sided focus on getting, an air of entitlement, impatience, and the unwillingness to invest for the long term. (This conversation didn't bode well for my talk, and the talk didn't go over well.)

Actions based on a tit-for-tat understanding of reciprocity—whether or not they are ethical—may achieve a short-run objective, but their power is exhausted with the attainment of the immediate result. As in the case of the business school alumni who felt no further obligation to the school beyond paying for their education, people who have been the targets of such practices will have no incentive to help in the future. The misuse of the reciprocity principle, then, adds nothing to our fund of social capital; it doesn't create new opportunities.

The lesson is that we cannot *pursue* the power of reciprocity. The deliberate pursuit of reciprocity fails, just like the pursuit of happiness: "To the extent to which one makes happiness the objective of his motivation," psychologist Viktor Frankl explains, "he necessarily makes it the object of his attention. But precisely by so doing he loses sight of the *reason for happiness*, and happiness itself must fade away."[18] When we try to invoke reciprocity directly, we lose sight of the reason for it: *helping others*. Paradoxically, it is in helping others without expecting reciprocity in return that we invoke the power of reciprocity. As shown in Figure 4.2, the path to reciprocity is indirect: reciprocity *ensues* from the social capital built by making contributions to others.[19]

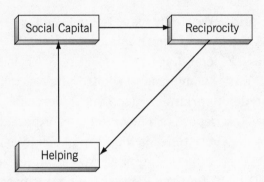

Figure 4.2. **Reciprocity Ensues from Contributions to Others**

Acts of contribution, big and small, build your fund of social capital, creating a vast *network of reciprocity.* A network of reciprocity reaches far and wide. And so those who help you may
not be those you help. The help you receive may come from distant corners of a network; it may come unbidden and unasked
for. Janet's story, related in Chapter One, describes the never-
ending waves of reciprocity she initiated by taking herself "out
of the equation"—helping others without regard to how they
might help her.

The same paradox holds for success and happiness. This is
the concrete reality behind the injunctions found in religious
wisdom like the New Testament's "give and ye shall receive."
As Ananda Coomaraswamy writes in *The Dance of Shiva,* "All
that is best for us comes of itself into our hands—but if we strive
to overtake it, it perpetually eludes us." Psychologist Viktor
Frankl makes the same point when he advises writers "to obey
their scientific and artistic conscience, as the case may be, and
not to care for success. Success and happiness *must happen,* the
less one cares for them, the more they can."[20] Similarly, the less
Janet cares about getting something in return, the more she allows reciprocity to happen. Like all the best networkers, she
practices *generalized* reciprocity, investing in the wider network
of reciprocity without expectation of getting anything in return.[21]

Her experience is that somewhere, somehow, someone turns up to help her when she needs it.

Each contribution you make is an addition to an endless chain of events; visualize it as a drop of rain rippling the water's surface, sending out wider and wider and wider rings of influence. By practicing generalized reciprocity—contributing to others without worrying about who will help you or how you will be helped—you invest in a vast network of reciprocity that will be there when you need it.

■ Investing Your Social Capital

Implicit in the discussion so far is the idea that service to others *invests* in the network of reciprocity. The two-person exchange of help and assistance is the basic building block of this network, and so your current relationships are natural focal points for making investments. By helping a member of your networks, you will invoke a reciprocal response. Indeed, whether or not you think it through to its logical end, when you help someone, you implicitly expect help in return—and you would be miffed if you didn't get it. But the issue turns on *why* you would help someone in the first place: is it to get something in return, or to genuinely help the other person? It's true that if you want something from someone, you should give to the person first.[22] For example, if you want information, give it first and the probability of reciprocity rises. But helping another person as a cold-hearted economic calculation of investments and rates of return doesn't elicit much of a response beyond a coldly calculated repayment. Helping another person simply because it's *the right thing to do*, without expecting repayment from the person, invests in the fund of social capital, and paradoxically generates reciprocity for you far beyond that available from calculated tit-for-tat exchanges. Hence, this chapter will focus on investing in relationships in the spirit of helping others for the sake of helping, without regard to being helped in return.

Investing in Your Relationships

What can you invest in a relationship? Your current personal and business networks contain a portfolio of possibilities. If you've built the kind of entrepreneurial networks described in Chapter Three, you have enriched your social capital. This boosts your ability to tap all sorts of once-hidden resources: information, ideas, leads, job openings, personnel, business opportunities, money, power and influence, emotional support, and more. Some of these resources are yours, such as knowledge you gleaned via your networks, and you can grant these resources directly. Other resources are those you know where to find, perhaps a member of your networks who has them or knows where or how to get them. As Samuel Johnson remarked, "Knowledge is of two kinds. We know a subject ourselves, or we know where we can find information upon it." The same is true for any resource: you have it, or know where to find it.

To whom should you contribute? As a start, consider the people you named in the sociometric survey in Chapter Two. Of course, you know and have contact with a much larger number of people, so that your list of candidates is much longer. And some of the best investments are spontaneous, created in the moment of a human encounter, rather than thought out in advance. Yet you have to start somewhere, and those you named in the survey are good candidates. Use Worksheet 4.1 to record names and possible contributions. This worksheet contains spaces for twenty names, the maximum possible in this book's sociometric survey. If you didn't have twenty names, add anyone who now occurs to you.

■ Worksheet 4.1. Investing in Your Relationships ■

Name	What the Person Needs
1.	
2.	
3.	
4.	
5.	
6.	
7.	
8.	
9.	
10.	
11.	
12.	
13.	
14.	
15.	
16.	
17.	
18.	
19.	
20.	

What should you contribute? My old adviser, psychologist Donald Schwartz, once told me that the best thing one could do for another person is to help the person meet his or her needs. You might be able to guess what a person needs, but the experiments discussed in Chapter Two demonstrate that most people cannot accurately predict even a spouse's or close peer's preferences. There's a *cognitive gap* in every relationship—interpersonal knowledge is incomplete even in close relationships. For example, I started studying Spanish a few years ago, after I had several occasions to visit Spain. I mentioned my language avocation to my close friend Rob Faulkner—who then spoke to me in Spanish! I had no idea he knew Spanish, even though he and I had known each other for twelve years, worked closely on several major projects, visit each other's homes, and talk and send e-mail incessantly. He was best man in my wedding. And yet I didn't know him as well as I thought. (Now our e-mail notes are peppered with Spanish phrases and slang.) Based on this lesson, I start with the working assumption that I don't really know anyone—spouse, friend, colleague, acquaintance, or stranger. This mental stance provides openings for breakthroughs in mutual understanding.

Given the cognitive gap in every relationship, you should assume that you don't really know what a person needs. Your task is to find out. Finding out requires active listening. It begins by engaging in a conversation where you listen to the person's words and meanings, and even observe body language. You play back what you thought you heard, and invite the person to respond, correct, or amend what you said. This is an iterative process that usually takes several rounds. Active listening is a skill that improves with practice.[23]

Your true intention matters—*why* are you are listening. Even active listening, notes Stephen Covey, can be motivated with the "intent to reply, to control, to manipulate."[24] Covey advocates what he calls *empathic listening*:

When I say empathic listening, I mean listening with the intent to *understand.* I mean *seeking first* to understand, to really understand. It's an entirely different paradigm.

Empathic (from *empathy*) listening gets inside another person's frame of reference. You look out through it, you see the world the way they see the world, you understand their paradigm, you understand how they feel.[25]

If we listen actively and with empathy we can start to bridge the cognitive gaps in our relationships. Doing so allows us to identify the kind of help the other person needs. Besides the specific help given, the mere act of helping invests in a relationship. Acts of help are empowering. Prior to getting the offer of a faculty position at the University of Michigan Business School, I spent a snowy month in Ann Arbor as part of a mutual getting-to-know-you effort. Kim Cameron was a professor of organizational behavior at Michigan. Kim and I had not met before, so the cognitive gap in our relationship was gargantuan. In the course of an informal conversation, Kim asked about my ongoing research. I thought that he was listening to judge; judging is a common academic mental stance, and the department had not yet made up its collective mind about the job offer. But I realize now, looking back, that he was listening to help. At one point, when I mentioned that I needed to find some managers to interview for a project, he asked, "How can I help you?" I was stunned. He meant it. I recovered my composure and asked if he knew anyone who fit the description of the type of managers I was looking to talk with. Kim thought for a moment. He responded with the names of several senior managers who were members of his business networks, offering to put me in touch with them. He closed structural holes in his networks (the disconnects between me and these managers) while he closed the cognitive gap between us by listening for my needs. Access to these managers was the resource I needed; interviewing them gave me information that helped me successfully conclude the project. It resulted in a publication in *Chief Executive* magazine.[26] But the real lesson of this story is the empowering effect of the act of helping. I have felt a positive connection to Kim ever since. And his act of helping contributed to my feeling that *this* was the kind of department I wanted to be a part of; if I received the offer, I vowed to accept it.

Creating Human Moments

The daily round of life brings everyone into contact with scores of people. Each face-to-face encounter, no matter how brief, is an opportunity to invest in the fund of social capital by creating what Edward Hallowell, M.D., calls "the human moment."

> What exactly is the human moment? The two prerequisites are (1) people's physical presence and (2) their attention. That's it. Two or more people together paying attention to one another create a human moment. Physical presence alone isn't enough; you can ride shoulder to shoulder with someone for ten hours in an airplane and not have a human moment the whole ride. And attention alone isn't enough; you can pay attention to someone over the telephone, but that is not a human moment.
>
> Human moments are powerful and require energy. This is why they should be used judiciously—rare is the person who can perform effectively in a human moment for hours on end! . . . The human moment can be brisk, businesslike, and brief. It does not have to be emotional or touchy-feely at all. A five-minute conversation can make all the difference in the world, if the parties participate actively. To make it work, you have to set aside what you're doing, put down the memo you were reading, disengage your laptop, abandon your day-dream, and bring your attention to bear upon the person you're with. Usually, when you do this, the other person (or people) will feel the energy and respond in kind, naturally. If they

don't, you will feel frustrated and disappointed. This is why human moments can be so draining, annoying, and counterproductive when they do not work well, and it is one reason many people avoid them. But if the other person (or people) does respond, then you are cooking. You quickly create a force field of exceptional power.[27]

The world needs more human moments, Hallowell argues, especially since so much communication today is electronic and asynchronous. Human moments require face-to-face conversation. Electronic media, such as e-mail, are efficient modes of communication, accelerating the transmission of routine information and improving its accuracy; these media can bring isolated people into contact with others.[28] Electronic media can even aid community-building efforts and increase face-to-face interactions.[29] But electronic technology is "impoverished in social cues and shared experience."[30] Experts agree that it is no substitute for the human moment created by face-to-face interaction. For example, electronic communication is not suited for building trust among strangers, or a true team out of people who have never met.[31] Prospective members of a team, for example, must meet face to face first; then electronic communication can assist the process of team-building.[32] As my colleague Judy Olson, an expert in electronic work, recommends in all cases, "You have to have dinner first."[33]

Electronic technology can help you stay in contact with colleagues, friends, and acquaintances. In addition to e-mail, services such as America Online and publications such as *Fast Company* magazine online make it easy to electronically clip a news item and forward it. Getting a valuable news item is always welcome, so sending it is an investment in a relationship. But electronic technology is not well-suited for making investments *over the long run* in your relationships. Eventually a strong relationship deteriorates on a steady diet of e-mail, voice mail, and faxes. Relying too much on technology leads to growing mis-interpretations, misunderstandings, and even suspicions and dis-trust.[34] As a divisional president of a large multidivisional firm told the other presidents at a regular monthly meeting that had been put off for three months, "When I see you on a regular basis, I trust you. When I haven't seen you, I start to distrust you." Human mo-ments must leaven the use of electronic communication.

Potential human moments abound; they surround us. Every human encounter is one, from a fleeting interaction with a store clerk to the people we pass in the hallways of workplaces to our most intimate relationships. Creating human moments is good business—see this chapter's case study. But turning *any* human encounter into a human moment invests in the fund of social capital. It can be as simple as greeting and acknowledging peo-ple in the daily round of life. Wofford College in Spartanburg, South Carolina, and Hampden-Sydney College in Hampden-Sydney, Virginia, have cultural traditions that promote the cre-ation of human moments, such as the simple act of greeting strangers on campus. Susan Wiley, a 1968 Michigan MBA who is a professor at Wofford College, described life at Wofford in these terms: "If you walked across our lovely campus on any day, nearly everyone would speak to you, even though you wouldn't know anyone." Jon Kjos, a 2000 Michigan MBA, told me about the same tradition at his college, Hampden-Sydney. Practices extend beyond greeting to introducing oneself and ask-ing if the stranger needs help. These practices are codified in the Hampden-Sydney guide to etiquette.[35] Their effect is empower-ing, for both the greeted and greeter. Such practices contribute to the building of strong emotional bonds, producing deeply loyal alumni.

Your physical presence and attention are all it takes to turn your next interaction with another person into a human moment.

Creating Human Moments and Doing Business

When Rob Faulkner was looking to buy a new place to live in Amherst, Massachusetts, he contacted Betsy Egan, a Realtor he had met at a Christmas party. She had a reputation as a excellent broker with a very satisfied clientele. Her interactions with Rob illustrate the combination of creating human moments and doing business.

"I arranged to meet Betsy at 9:00 on Monday," Rob says. "She was engaged, focused, and asked a bunch of great questions about me, my life, my plans—all the while running down the pluses and minuses of the places we were going to see. The dominant tone was, simply, I'm here to help you find the place you will love."

After viewing a few places, Betsy suggested that Rob see a condo called Amity Place. "I had just heard about this place from a lunch engagement with another of my friends who had taken a look," says Rob. "It was an expensive condo, but, hey, what the heck, it might be fun." They arranged to meet at Amity Place late that afternoon.

Rob says he had no intention of buying the condo. But Betsy had listened carefully to his needs and tastes, and then matched him with the right place. "I fell in love with it," Rob says. "Betsy handled this all with a very light touch. She said, 'The place sells itself, Rob.' And indeed it did. Again, her focus was on showing me something I would fall in love with, absolutely."

Over the next three days, Betsy and Rob communicated at least three times a day. "She ever so nicely mentioned a banker as someone I 'should check with and talk to,' but I wasn't even sure why at this point. When I talked to him," Rob recalls, "I realized that he too was at the same Christmas party where I met Betsy! He told me how I could swing the whole loan on the Amity Place condo."

"Betsy drew me into her circle of friends," Rob notes. "These ties facilitate trust—in the banker, in Betsy, in Amity Place, and even in myself. They are brokers, to be sure, but I was clearly being treated as a friend, a partner, and as someone whom they were helping. This may sound rather naive in the light of the literature on principals, agents, and third parties, but the phenomenology of it is very, very different when you are in the actual doing of the deal. Moreover, it was fun!"

Betsy also introduced Rob to the lawyer he needed to represent his side of the transaction. The deal went through smoothly, and Rob moved into his new home. Betsy bought Rob a serving dish as a home-warming gift. Her real estate firm sent champagne and flowers, and followed up a week later with a customer feedback questionnaire.

Rob summarized his experience with Betsy: "Clearly here is someone who likes people, likes to help them, understands them, and not only 'talks the talk' and 'walks the walk' but does the deal in such a way that I came away learning a whole lot about the business, myself, and my new life with the condo that, sure enough, I fell in love with. It sold itself because Betsy allowed me to see something I would otherwise not have even considered possible, reasonable, or affordable. She gave me as much time as I needed to talk, no matter what the subject. She gave me access to her network. Ties of ties led to an expansion of my horizons and, well, opportunities. At no time did I ever, ever perceive that I was being treated as a babe in the woods, as part of a 'deal,' or as an occasion for raking in some fees. The entire chain of events was marked by graciousness, humor, helpfulness, and serious advice about who to call next and with whom to deal in the unfolding sequence of events. Betsy's network created an atmosphere of concern and help, turning this into something of a special event for them, too."

Source: Interview with Rob Faulkner.

Investing in Your Affiliations

Just as we invest in our interpersonal relationships, we can invest in those associations, groups, and organizations with which we are affiliated. Many nonprofits, for example, have pressing needs for contributions of time and services, as well as goods and money. Contributing your personal resources, such as volunteering to staff an event or serve on a committee, is an investment in the fund of social capital. So are contributions of corporate resources for worthy causes, such as giving employees time off for charitable work, granting money or financing scholarships, donating supplies, or arranging for the free use of corporate facilities and equipment. For example, HUMAX Corporation offers its Web-administered network assessment tool at a deep discount for educational purposes, such as use in courses on networks and social capital, and for doctoral research. You may be in a position to influence the allocation of corporate resources. At the least, your entrepreneurial networks can help you to identify worthy causes and communicate their needs to those who make allocation decisions.

How do you start? Consider the outside affiliations you listed in the sociometric survey in Chapter Two. List them by name in Worksheet 4.2. This worksheet contains ten rows, corresponding to the ten types of affiliations you were asked about. Copy this worksheet if you need more space.

■ Worksheet 4.2. Investing in Your Affiliations ■	
Name of Association	What the Association Needs
1.	
2.	
3.	
4.	
5.	
6.	
7.	
8.	
9.	
10.	

What does each one need? Cognitive gaps exist here, just as they do in every interpersonal relationship. You should assume that you don't really know what an outside affiliation needs. Your task is to find out, using the same active, empathic listening described earlier. Inquire about needs at the next organized event or meeting. Or arrange to meet with an officer, director, or representative, and begin your inquiry there in a face-to-face human moment.

Filling Structural Holes

By building entrepreneurial networks, you create natural opportunities to make investments. An entrepreneurial network is an *opportunity network:* every structural hole, gap, or disconnect represents opportunities to create value by linking people. Some holes are easy to fill; attempting to fill others entangles you in the network dilemma described in the introduction to this chapter and depicted in Figure 4.1. Did you decide to use the union or disunion strategy? In the long run, the union strategy is likely to invoke the power of reciprocity. The disunion strategy would not. It could even backfire—if the customer ever finds out that you knew of a better alternative, not only would you harm your relationship with this customer but it's likely that the customer would tell others about your behavior. In my experience, most devout disunion strategists are eventually discovered and dismissed as unabashed opportunists. Of course, there is no guarantee that the beneficiary of your union strategy will reciprocate in some way, or that news of your good deed will net you benefits in return. Like all worthwhile investments, investing in social capital carries risk. The union strategy, however, is the prescription for long-term success. Those who adopt the union strategy as their modus operandi build a productive culture of cooperation, trust, and reciprocity, continuously creating value for their customers, coworkers, organizations, and themselves.

Please note that I'm not advocating career suicide. Sometimes the wise decision is to follow the sales dictum "you sell what you have" until the company improves its products or you find another job. In some companies, losing a sale by choosing the union strategy is considered an act of disloyalty, and puts your job or promotion prospects at risk. A company's incentive system may make it virtually impossible for employees to choose the union strategy. If you are measured and rewarded only for short-term financial success, you will be hard-pressed to choose the union strategy; you will feel compelled to sacrifice the future for the present. Effective managers, however, don't punish the loss of a sale due to the union strategy. They know that the union strategy builds customer loyalty in the long run, and invokes the power of reciprocity. They recognize a lost sale as a source of feedback about customers and products. Instead of chastising a salesperson who lost a sale but won the gratitude of a future customer, good managers use the feedback to improve products, pricing, promotion, and packaging. These forward-looking management practices, I regret, are not common.

Shortsighted organizational policies and practices deprive both the individual and the company of the power of reciprocity. In cases like this, the problem is more the organization's fault than the individual's. In Chapter Five, I'll talk about the organization's role in building social capital. Here I'll stick to what we *can* do, given the opportunities and constraints of our environments.

It's not always possible to neatly separate *building* social capital from *using* it; often, the two occur simultaneously. Many of the practices for building social capital reviewed in Chapter Three also involve using social capital. The practices described in this chapter, however, focus more specifically on the use-of-capital side. They illustrate the range of possibilities, including examples of practices used by free agents and by organization members. There are, of course, countless other practices. Adapt these practices for your own use, or use them as a spur to thinking about new practices.

#1. Staying in communication. Keeping in touch with the members of your networks allows you to learn about hole-filling possibilities. For example, networking expert Susan RoAne reports a practice used by her friend Bill Gillis. As he describes, "I use 'keeping in touch' cards and I make it a practice to send a few each month. Through the recent use of these cards, I was able to match an East Coast business ethics group and a West Coast anesthesiologist. The ethics group needed a minority member and my physician friend wanted to be more active in business. The doctor is now on their board."[36]

Here's an example of a similar practice in an entirely different sphere, global geopolitics. When George Bush was president of the United States, he regularly sent personalized notes to people all over the United States and world, as part of his efforts to invest in these personal relationships. Journalists at the time called him "the retail president" for this practice. By staying in communication, he was better able to build consensus on domestic and international issues, and to resolve crises by bringing together conflicting parties.[37]

#2. Making introductions. The simple act of introducing two people closes a network gap. As described above, Kim Cameron filled a structural hole by introducing me to the managers he knew. Because they trusted Kim and he vouched for me, they freely shared information about managerial practices and company policies with a stranger, me. Betsy Egan filled two holes by introducing Rob Faulkner to a banker and a lawyer (this chapter's case study). Introductions don't have to be elaborate or formal, as these cases illustrate. These cases also illustrate, however, that introductions are deliberate acts to help others by filling structural holes.

#3. Responding to introductions and requests. The counterpart of making introductions is responding to them, and granting requests to help a third party. For example, the managers I met through Kim responded to his request to help me. Sociologist

Brian Uzzi describes a similar case among suppliers and manufacturers in the New York garment industry:

> One CEO explained how [a] tie formed between him and a manufacturer called "Diana." He said that his contact with Diana began when Norman, a close business friend of his and Diana's, asked him "to help Diana out" in a time of need (cut her fabric at a special price and time), even though he had no prior contact with her. . . . [The CEO said] "So why did I help her out? Because Norman asked 'Help her out'."[38]

Responding to introductions and granting requests both make a double investment: in the relationship with the person who makes the introduction, and in the relationship with the third-party beneficiary. Double investments grow the fund of social capital multiplicatively, as compounding interest grows a financial fund.

#4. Hosting and participating in informal gatherings. Informal gatherings come in all shapes and sizes. For example, Cisco Systems engineering consultant Ed Vielmetti, mentioned in Chapter Three, hosts a monthly dinner in Ann Arbor, inviting various members of his networks. He participates in a similar dinner gathering each month in San Francisco, coordinating his travel and work schedule to coincide with it. At AT&T fifteen years ago, Allan Ditchfield started an informal gathering known as "Donuts with Ditch." He exported this practice when he moved to MCI, and then again when he became chief information officer of insurance provider Progressive Corporation, where I first made contact with him.[39] A Donuts-with-Ditch session takes place every two weeks, for about two or three hours. He invites no more than ten employees to each session; most are chosen at random, but some ask to be invited if they have an issue to raise. Trust is critical. "I have a rule—it's a sacred open door—that there will be no retaliation," Allan says. "No one's going to get

hurt by [what they say]. I don't tell management." These sessions are natural venues for filling structural holes between levels and groups.

#5. Holding formal meetings. Formal meetings are often misery and wastes of time. In well-run meetings, however, decisions are made, there is little decision rework, the quality of decisions is good, and participants actually enjoy themselves; my colleague John Tropman has written a book that explains how meetings can accomplish these results.[40] Given the trend toward teams and group work, formal meetings can't be avoided—and they shouldn't be, from a networking point of view. Formal meetings can be powerful vehicles for filling structural holes— but only if attendees are carefully selected to include people from across levels, departments, and locations. If they include those inside an organizational clump, formal meetings only solidify clumpiness. GE's famous Work-Out sessions are excellent examples of formal meetings that fill structural holes and produce concrete results. Seven steps implement a Work-Out; quoting from *The GE Way Fieldbook*:[41]

1. Choose issues to discuss.
2. Select a cross-functional team appropriate for the problem.
3. Choose a "champion" who will see any Work-Out recommendations through to implementation.
4. Let the team meet for 3 days (or 2½), drawing up recommendations to improve your company's success.
5. Meet with managers who can say on the spot "Yes," or "No," or "I'll get on to that" (with further study time specified) to each recommendation.
6. Hold more meetings as required to pursue the implementation of the recommendations.
7. Keep the process going, with these and other issues.

#6. Bridging internal organizational clumps. The design of an organization, as discussed in Chapter Three, creates numerous

structural holes and hence opportunities to fill them. For example, many job vacancies in organizations are filled internally; the problem, of course, is linking the vacancy with the internal candidate. That's where we can fill holes. About 25 percent of internal job vacancies are filled by interpersonal referrals; these referrals fill the hole between a person looking to hire someone and the prospective job candidate.[42] In today's work world, people often have multiple accountabilities, reporting to two or more bosses who work in different locations, teams, functions, or departments. These arrangements can be sources of stress— or opportunities to fill the gap between the bosses. Sometimes, filling holes must take place outside prescribed corporate guidelines and policies, as Intel corporate entrepreneurs did as they pursued the ultimately successful RISC (Reduced Instruction Set Computing) project.[43] Other times, corporate entrepreneurs close gaps by working within official policies. For example, Harvard Business School professor Rosabeth Moss Kanter describes how an internal entrepreneur filled holes between the organizational clumps of sales, service, and product development: "He first wrote a memo to all of the sales people in his area, copying the district managers for service and products. . . . He then held a series of sales meetings, inviting commercial and service staff too. . . . [He] explained and reexplained the benefits of cooperation across the sales/service/products boundaries to people from each function."[44]

Rich Nastasi, head of the systems group at General Electric's Retailer Financial Services, filled holes in a bid to cut the time it took to "convert" a new retailer from an applicant to an online customer. "A small cross-functional team mapped the typical process, which was taking an average of eight weeks. Nastasi then brought together a group of systems, marketing, finance, and customer service people and challenged them to complete new customer conversions in a matter of days, not weeks."[45] It worked; average conversion time fell to a week.

Similarly, AlliedSignal CEO Larry Bossidy arranges organizational structure to fill holes between departmental clumps: "Organizationally, I pair marketing with technology so that I can make sure that they are working together. In the past, the marketing people were working on what they wanted to, and the technology people were working on what they wanted to, and the products never got to the market on time."[46]

#7. Bridging external organizational boundaries. The organization's networks of customers, suppliers, and alliances are full of structural holes, and hence natural opportunities to create value by filling them. For example,

> A corporate entrepreneur saw an opportunity to connect two of his major suppliers while developing a new medical products business. One manufacturer, in the south, had cheap labor costs and good employee morale, but was nonetheless losing money due to lack of business. The other, in the north, had high labor costs and an employee shortage. By introducing these two manufacturers the venture manager reduced the costs of one and increased the sales of the other.[47]

The same hole-filling practices apply at all levels. For example, AT&T Global Information Solutions (the old NCR) encouraged the formation of new ties among its 125 alliance partners by bringing them together in its Global Alliance Conference.[48] Similarly, thousands of customers, executives, and strategic allies attend Compaq's annual Innovate Forum.[49]

#8. Using the Internet and the Web to fill holes and make the world small. The Internet and the World Wide Web provide unprecedented opportunities to bridge structural holes, no matter where they may be. For example, John Agno, president of Signature, devised the Internet-based Dealer-to-Dealer Network (DDN) to fill structural holes in the personal and organizational assessment tool industry. This industry, as John explained to me,

is quite fragmented, containing many small assessment tool publishers who sell via many small independent dealers. These dealers sell through their personal networks in their local areas. "The small business dealer," John says, "feels very alone due to little marketing support from the assessment tool publisher. Most dealers receive few sales leads outside their personal networks and have difficulty in servicing clients with multiple locations outside the dealer's geographical location." John uses the electronic DDN to unite these heretofore disconnected dealers: "DDN communication consists of a weekly e-mail newsletter which includes dealer requests, concerns, geographical sales referral opportunities, sales prospecting techniques, industry articles, product reviews, best business practices, resolving distribution channel conflicts and satisfied client references. Through the DDN, dealers can confidentially carry on conversations that share knowledge and resolve the problems/opportunities of the day."

How well does the DDN work? Here are examples of holes filled via the DDN: a local dealer in Houston, Texas, arranges to have an assessment performed for a client who has a job candidate in Tampa, Florida; a dealer in San Francisco closes a deal with a national construction company with references provided by other dealers who have worked elsewhere with the construction industry; a dealer in the Southeast uses the DDN to contact a publisher's management to help resolve an outstanding dispute; and a dealer polls the DDN to find an assessment tool for measuring corporate stress that a prospective client wants to use.

■

These eight practices, ranging from making introductions to tapping the technological power of the Internet and Web, are methods for filling structural holes. Where should you start? Which holes should you fill? Your current networks contain lots of fillable holes. Examine the people and needs that you recorded in Worksheet 4.1, along with your outside affiliations and their needs, which you recorded in Worksheet 4.2. Consider each and every possible pair of people, and the value that could be created by connecting them. How could you bring the two people together—a casual introduction, formal meeting, or some other method of filling holes? Similarly, consider each and every possible pair of outside affiliations, asking the same questions. You can even consider crossing these two, matching each person with each outside affiliation.

To be systematic, use Worksheet 4.3 to record names and possible linkages. Assign each person (or outside affiliation) to a row *and* its corresponding column. For example, if you write

■ Worksheet 4.3. Filling Holes in Your Networks ■			
	1	2	3	4
1				
2				
3				
4				

Bob's name in column one, you should also write his name in row one. If you write Sue's name in column two, you should also write her name in row two. Each cell in the matrix represents a possible connection between two people. If the two people are strangers, would it help them to meet each other? If the two already know each other, how could you reinforce their link? For illustration, consider the partially completed worksheet in Figure 4.3. Then, complete your Worksheet 4.3 by writing in each cell how you could fill holes in your networks.

Note: Due to space limitations on the printed page, this worksheet contains room for only a limited number of names. Make copies for considering more people, as well as for considering interconnections among your outside affiliations.

	Bob	Sue	George	
Bob		I invite Bob and Sue to join a new task force.	I invite Bob and George to my monthly "open house" dinner.	
Sue			I include Sue and George in my eGroups on the Web.	
George				

Figure 4.3. An Example of Worksheet 4.3 in Use

■ Networking Total Quality Management: Using a Personal Quality Checklist

Using your social capital, like building it, may seem a daunting task. If it feels that way to you, remember the wisdom of small wins. You don't have to change your entire lifestyle in one fell swoop. Small changes, small wins can yield big payoffs. Using a personal quality checklist can help you to make small wins a routine of life.

I learned about personal quality checklists from my University of Chicago colleague Harry Roberts, a statistician and expert on total quality management (TQM). Harry had met Bernie Sergesketter, then a vice president at AT&T, when Tink Campbell (president of the Chicago Presidents Organization) closed a structural hole by inviting each of them to speak at a Quality Forum. They joined forces to write a practical book on personal quality checklists.[50] Harry and Bernie acknowledge that they didn't invent the idea of the personal quality checklist; Benjamin Franklin gets that credit. But the two perfected the idea by combining it with modern TQM concepts and tools. The result is a simple, easy-to-use, amazingly powerful tool for improving personal quality. You can use it to manage the processes of building and using networks.

The heart of the checklist idea is the concept of a *defect*. A defect is a shortcoming or lapse in one's key personal processes. A defect is a failure to meet a standard, such as responding to letters in five business days or being on time for meetings. Each defect is counted and recorded on a personal quality checklist like the one in Worksheet 4.4, which tracks defects day by day for a week. Customarily, the information generated from the weekly checklists is then plotted on a time-series or run chart showing the total number of defects per week. (The horizontal dimension of the chart is time in weeks, and the vertical dimension is total number of defects per week.) However, you could simply record the total number of defects per week on a piece of paper, in a spreadsheet, in your Palm Pilot, or whatever method

■ Worksheet 4.4. Personal Quality Checklist for Networking ■

Your Name _____

Networking Productivity Checklist: Week of _____

Defect Category	Sunday	Monday	Tuesday	Wednesday	Thursday	Friday	Saturday	Total

Source: Adapted with the permission of The Free Press, a Division of Simon & Schuster, Inc., from *Quality Is Personal: A Foundation for Total Quality Management* by Harry V. Roberts and Bernard F. Sergesketter. Copyright © 1993 by Harry V. Roberts and Bernard F. Sergesketter.

works for you. The idea is to keep track of your defects, and to look for an upward or downward trend over time. Take a quick look now at Worksheet 4.4 so that you get an idea of what a checklist looks like. Then return to the text and consider the concrete process of constructing a checklist and using it to manage networking productivity.

Why count defects? Some people think it's too negative, arguing that we should count the number of times we do things right. But the wisdom of counting defects is based on TQM, psychology, and lots of experience with checklists. "Fortunately," Harry and Bernie say, "most of us do things right much more often than we do things wrong, so it is easier in practice to count the defects." If you don't have any defects in a week, then you don't have to record anything. "Moreover, we can get positive satisfaction from avoiding defects—witness accident prevention programs that count days without accidents."[51] Their experience shows that making a checklist and counting defects produce immediate small wins: no or few defects in the first weeks! Why? The act of making a well-constructed checklist produces a powerful motivational effect. For example, consider Harry's initial experience with his five-standard checklist:

> If, unbeknown to Roberts, a guardian angel had been keeping track of defects in these five standards *before* he started his checklist, there would have been *many* defects in these five standards. But once the checklist was in his pocket, there was a remarkable change of behavior. The list was a continuing reminder of new standards that had to be satisfied or defects would be recorded. He realized that with a little effort, he could literally *prevent* most defects in these standards.
>
> The checklist was an almost magical device that calmed him down, made him resist the temptation to try to do everything at once, shuffle madly to find what to do next, and in general create chaos on the desk. [For example], during the first week, the desk went from cluttered to clean.[52]

When I started experimenting with a personal quality checklist, I put only one standard on it: "Office is one iota neater after each use." Like most academics, I worked in the midst of a shambles of old papers, files, articles, and books. Like most, I harbored the dream of taking a whole day to come in and straighten it all out. That day never came. The checklist replaced this illusion of "batch processing" with the concept of continuous improvement: Every day I came in, I had to make my office a little cleaner. There was no final deadline—no ultimate state of cleanliness—which turned out to be empowering. My office had to be only one iota neater. An iota isn't much. I found that in one minute I could sift through a pile of old papers and toss out all or most of it; that was all I had to do for a single day's visit. I produced zero defects in the first two weeks. Then, defects slowly began to mount up again.

Defects are opportunities for learning and improvement, because each defect raises two questions, "Why did it occur?" and "How can a recurrence be prevented?"[53] "Why" and "how" led in a series of steps to root causes and then back up to satisfactory remedies. I figured out that I had picked most of the low-hanging fruit—those piles of old papers. Why was my office still messy? I noticed that I brought junk mail to my office, adding to the mess. Since the standard was one iota neater, I had to tidy up even more to compensate for the added junk-mail mess. So I started sorting my mail in the faculty mail room, tossing out junk mail, and even taking care of small tasks right then and there. Eventually, however, I hit rock bottom: defects every day. The root cause, I learned, was that I didn't have a real filing *system*. I had always thought that I didn't file properly because I was "disorganized." The real reason, I realized, was that I simply didn't know how to set one up. That realization led to a huge breakthrough in personal quality.

I tell you the details of my experience so that you can see an example of how a checklist is used over time to boost personal quality. It continually produces small wins, occasionally big breakthroughs. To construct a checklist for networking productivity, you need to produce four to six networking standards; never more than ten. Each standard should be simple, specific, measurable, and "operator controllable," meaning that you control it. The content of each standard will vary from person to person, depending on individual needs and objectives. Here are ten examples with some descriptions. Use or customize these categories; create your own. Write each of your standards in the space provided on Worksheet 4.4 and track the results. Ideally, one should make using checklists a lifelong habit. To get started, however, I recommend that you commit to a two-month trial period. After that, you may want to revise your networking standards and refine your checklist.

1. *Failure to convert a human encounter into a human moment.* Greeting my neighbors when I see them; speaking briefly with any acquaintance I run into; giving my undivided time and attention to colleagues upon request; saying hello to a clerk or toll taker.
2. *Failure to reconnect with an old contact once a week.* Old contact means someone I haven't seen, spoken with, or heard from in over six months; any method of reconnection is acceptable (phone, mail, e-mail). This is a weekly objective, so a defect isn't recorded until Friday.
3. *Missed opportunity to fill a structural hole.* Introducing two people soon after I see that value could be created by doing so; inviting the right people to my meetings; responding to requests from others to help a third party.
4. *Failure to share information.* Clipping a news item and sending it someone who could use it; keeping people informed of events, changes, news, and so on.
5. *Delayed return of phone call, e-mail message, or letter.* Failure to act at the first opportunity; failure to respond quickly with

a brief acknowledgment if there isn't enough time for a lengthy reply.

6. *Late for meetings.* Harry Roberts says that being late by even one second is a defect; he recommends always carrying reading or work materials in case others are late.[54]

7. *Failure to attend association meetings.* Attending annual conferences; attending monthly chapter meetings; attending special events.

8. *Failure to send thank you notes.* Failure to act at the first available opportunity; written notes preferred, electronic acceptable.

9. *Canceling lunch appointments.* Canceling lunch appointments that I've made or committed to; includes informal lunches with friends and formal business luncheons.

10. *Delayed updating of contact manager.* Failure to record new contact information, or update old information, at first available opportunity.

Personal quality checklists work, but they don't do the work for you. Checklists are only aids to using social capital. You have to do the work. Using your social capital—with or without checklists—requires a change of behavior on your part. Recall the advice from the end of Chapter Three: The goal is not to network harder, but smarter. Continual small wins over time, like regular deposits in a savings account, will accumulate into a social capital fortune.

■ Request and Receive

If we've invested in the fund of social capital by using our networks in service of others, then we can request help when we need it and expect to get it. Indeed, the less we've pursued the power of reciprocity, the more we can count on it; the more we've contributed to others without expecting anything in return, the more we can draw on the fund of social capital when the need arises. This is why it's always important to build and use our networks before we need them; if we've waited until we need help, it's too late.

For those who practice the philosophy in this book, help often arrives without explicit requests. Having needs met without request is so common for those who unselfishly contribute to others that networking experts Donna Fisher and Sandy Vilas give it a label: the "boomerang effect."[55] Like a boomerang, the help we give comes back to us, though in a roundabout way. For example, recall from Chapter One the story of Janet, the super-productive bank loan officer, who stopped trying to make loans and simply sought to help others, no matter what form the help might be. She makes more loans now than ever before, because all the people she helped send their friends, acquaintances, and contacts who need bank loans to see her. Janet never requests these referrals; they are made voluntarily—and with gratitude— by the people she helps.

Stephanie Wargo, an organizational studies major at the University of Michigan, was looking for a job, but she got it by "accident"—by using her networks for a purpose unrelated to her job search. As part of our course on social capital, students undertake a project designed to demonstrate the small-world principle. I assign a "target" person to each student team, someone whom they don't know, along with the objective of getting a dozen folders delivered by hand to this person. The team starts each folder by giving it to someone they think can forward it in a chain of contacts toward the target. In Stephanie's case, the target was my colleague Bob Holmes, director of human resource development at the University of Michigan. Stephanie told me what happened:

> I gave one of my small-world folders to my aunt, who works
> for the university and actually knew Robert Holmes. She was

really excited about the whole project and thought it was great that she could help the folder reach the target. Shortly after we conducted our small world experiment, my aunt was having lunch with a good friend and she was telling her about our experiment and how I was in a class about networking. Her friend is the vice president of human resources at KeyBank in downtown Ann Arbor and just happened to be looking for an intern for next semester. She said "Hey, might as well network!" So, through my aunt, I got in touch with the VP of human resources at KeyBank and got the job!

You can count on the power of reciprocity without making explicit requests. But making requests is an essential part of the process of using social capital. A request is a clear, concise, and honest expression of a need for help. It is not a demand. It is not an order. It is not an expression of entitlement. A request is made without the expectation of receiving help. As Donna Fisher and Sandy Vilas aptly put it, "A request that includes a hidden agenda, expectation, or manipulation is not a powerful, productive request. Even though people may respond to this type of request, they will not experience the trust and empowerment that is important in building strong networking relationships. Make requests, not demands, and people will be empowered and respond with true enthusiasm."[56]

You can make requests of those you've helped directly, or those you have not but who participate in the larger network of reciprocity. Requests can be made for specific resources from a person—time, advice, emotional support, assistance, business leads, money, and so forth—or for access to a person's networks where the resources reside. It's OK to make unreasonable requests, as long as you don't have any expectations about having them met. Unreasonable requests, like stretch goals, often enable others to go beyond their real or imagined limitations.

Requests take various forms, ranging from a human moment to an e-mail note to a public announcement in a group setting, even to a direct mail campaign if handled properly. Consider these examples:

- *Personal request for help and emotional support.* A professor who was suffering from a progressive illness, found it more and more difficult to continue her teaching.[57] "I was on medications and increasingly ill and finally I called a friend and senior colleague on a Sunday and I said, 'You have to help me figure out how to quit doing what I am doing. I can't do it another day.'" Her friend and colleague responded to her request with compassion and assistance, spending the afternoon with her, reassigning her students, taking care of all the paperwork, and attending to other details.

- *E-mail request for information.* Michael Crescenzi, a consultant at Deloitte Consulting and a former MBA student of mine at the University of Michigan, needed information about government contracts with suppliers. He contacted a former classmate from Michigan who had worked for the Navy writing such contracts. His classmate readily shared the information he had, but also put Michael in touch with a friend. This friend gave Michael information over the phone, and followed up with an e-mail message directing him to the Department of Defense Web site, which is used by contractors who are drafting government contracts. "Between the verbal information and going to that Web site, which would have been tough to find via search engines," Michael said, "I was able to gather the knowledge that was necessary for the assignment in about a tenth of the time it would have taken me by meandering along the Web."

- *Public request in a group setting.* Sandra Xenakis, a publicity specialist retained by HUMAX Corporation, announced her business services at one of our social capital seminars. During a break, another participant arranged to have lunch with her, and hired Sandra to manage her company's publicity campaign. Similarly, at a Manhattan meeting of Webgrrls, the networking group described in Chapter Three, a member announced that her husband was looking for a Web site designer for his company, the National Academy of Television Arts and Sciences. Another member, a Web site designer, approached her after the meeting; they went immediately to meet the woman's husband, and she was hired to design the Academy's Web page.[58]

- *Making requests via direct mail.* Lindsay Armishaw, managing director of Armishaw International Limited in New Zealand, used direct mail to help his friend Murray Cruickshank find venture capital for Murray's new horticultural product venture, EcoCover—a revolutionary, biodegradable mulch mat made from recycled rubbish. The two drafted a letter and RSVP mechanism, which they mailed to select people in Lindsay's network. The result? Lindsay describes, "Murray's goal was to find fifty-four shareholders who would own 60 percent of his company. The personalized letter was sent to about 25 percent of my network and resulted in the project being oversubscribed." Lindsay also included direct mail as a way to build a volunteer distribution network for *Grapevine Magazine,* a popular, independent community-based not-for-profit publication. *Grapevine's* mission is "to promote stable, loving relationships—to tackle family hurts and headaches in a positive, helpful way . . . to inject fun, hope and wholeness into homes all over the country." Lindsay describes the process: "I began phoning friends in churches across the city, speaking at groups, mail dropping, meeting with key individuals who had the ability to oversee a region, coordinate a sector, or manage an individual route." In nine months, *Grapevine* had two thousand enthusiastic volunteers who, at no cost, were more reliable than previously used commercial distributors.

■

Finally, close the loop: Report back on the results of people's honoring your requests. If someone helped you, acknowledge the help and let the person know of the outcome. If someone filled a structural hole for you, let both parties know what happened.

It is possible to summarize the process of using social capital in only four words: invest, request, receive, acknowledge.

CHAPTER SUMMARY

Closing a structural hole—bringing members of a network together when it's in their mutual interest—is often a better alternative than keeping the opportunity secret, even if it means an immediate loss for yourself to do so. It activates the principle of *reciprocity,* one of the most powerful principles in human society and the mainspring of networks. At all levels, from the interpersonal to the international, we get help because we help others. The paradox is that the less we worry about reciprocity, the more we get it; the more we contribute to others without expectation of repayment, the more we are repaid in the future.

Using social capital is more about investing than requesting; more about giving than getting. By building entrepreneurial networks, we boost our ability to discover and tap all sorts of resources that we can invest. Because there is a natural cognitive gap in every relationship, listening actively and with empathy is critical to understanding how we can invest social capital. Personal quality checklists help to manage the processes of building and using networks, making small wins a routine way of life.

If you've invested in the fund of social capital, you can count on the power of reciprocity without making explicit requests. Making requests, however, is an essential part of the process of using social capital. A request is a clear, concise, honest expression of a need for help; it is made without an expectation of receiving help. There are several forms of requests: personal requests, e-mail requests, public requests, and direct mail requests.

This chapter completes the three-part cycle of evaluating, building, and using social capital. The final step is to consider how social capital can be built as an organizational competence, the subject of Chapter Five.

Building Social Capital as an Organizational Competence

To this point I've talked about social capital in terms of individuals—specifically how you can evaluate, build, and invest your own social capital. Now I'll broaden the focus to take in entire organizations. There may have been a time when social capital was not an essential organizational competence (though it's hard to imagine the circumstances in which it would not have been useful, at the very least), but today it is vital. Massive changes—escalating needs for information and learning, pressing demands for innovation and creativity, continuous improvement, the shift toward flat and fluid organizational designs, and tighter integration of the organization with networks of customers, suppliers, and competitors—all demand that leaders build social capital as a distinctive organizational competence. But most leaders, as Stanford Business School professor Jeffrey Pfeffer concludes, are "looking for success in all the wrong places"—smart executives, big strategy, large size, being in the right industry, or economies of scale.[1] He warns

> If you seek success in the wrong places, you are likely to waste a lot of effort, focus on the wrong things, and, in the end, overlook some of the real sources of competitive leverage—the culture and capabilities of your organization that derive from how you manage your people. This is a more important source of sustained success than many of those so commonly mentioned, because it is much more difficult to imitate or understand capability and systems of management practice than it is to copy strategy, technology, or even global presence.[2]

In this chapter, you'll see how to look for success in one of the right places: building the personal and business networks of the people you lead. As Noel Tichy and Ram Charan prescribe, "The role of the leader is to *architect* these networks in a way that will lead to success in tomorrow's environment."[3] The lessons of this chapter apply to leaders at all levels, not just top executives. No matter where you are in the organization, no matter how big or small your group is, you can be the architect of social capital, helping yourself by helping others build their social capital.

The notion of helping others build their social capital leads directly to the paradox of empowerment. There may be things that one can compel others to do, but building social capital isn't one of them. Social capital involves qualities of sincere interest in others and genuineness in interactions. Somehow we have to facilitate others' efforts to build their social capital without trying to *make* them do so. Before considering the specific things one can do, take a moment to consider the paradoxical nature of empowering leadership.

■ The Paradox of Empowerment

Building social capital as an organizational competence requires constructing an environment that encourages and enables people to act in ways that create, maintain, and extend networks. That can mean intervening—sometimes drastically—to change the way people work and interrelate. But it also means stepping back to let empowerment take root, grow, and thrive. This is the *paradox of empowerment:* Empowerment means taking control and letting go at the same time.[4]

Taking control and letting go appear contradictory. Indeed, the paradox of empowerment traps many leaders who cannot accept or live with the contradiction. These leaders become either *abdicators* or *meddlers.* Those who embrace and thrive on the paradox become *coaches.* They are the leaders who learn how to build social capital as an organizational competence.

Abdicators let go but don't take control. They talk empowerment with great enthusiasm and energy, but forsake their responsibility to intervene and make deep changes in the organization's design and culture. It's still business as usual, despite the hoopla about empowerment. The CEO of a large Chicago bank, for example, declared 1992 the "Year of Empowerment" but didn't do anything—reengineer work processes, reorganize into teams, knock down functional walls, or revamp the incentive system—to make it happen. Years later, the bank remained a dysfunctional assortment of silos.

Abdicators have good intentions, but good intentions aren't enough. For example, I've worked with a CEO of a large multidivisional firm who *wants* his people to burst boundaries and build bridges across divisions. He has paid for expensive management seminars and extravagant outdoor leadership adventures. Seminars and adventures inspire, boost camaraderie, and spark new ideas. But after they're over, everyone goes back and hits the same wall: an incentive system that encourages cutthroat behavior between divisions and punishes cooperation across divisional lines. The CEO fears to change this system. Until he does, his good intentions will never become reality.

Meddlers take control but can't let go. They're willing to make changes, but they can't step back and let empowerment bloom. In their heart of hearts, they fear empowerment and the development of social capital. Often, they hold a bleak view of human nature, believing that people naturally dislike work and shirk responsibility.[5] Meddlers are a little suspicious of what Douglas McGregor calls the human needs "for belonging, for association, for acceptance by one's fellows, for giving and receiving friendship and love."[6] They fear that allowing workers to form their own networks will create groups or factions that are hostile to management's interests. Hence, workers must be controlled, coerced, and manipulated. So meddlers attempt to micromanage the processes of building networks. They try to force people to build networks that the managers can oversee, control, and direct, rather than creating conditions that allow networks to blossom and thrive on their own.

Coaches thrive on the paradox of empowerment. They take control *and* let go. The leader-as-coach sets the game plan—mission, goals, vision, values, and strategies—making deep changes in organization design to create an environment in which networks flourish, both inside and outside the organization. Leaders who understand coaching provide all the support their people need. But coaches know the difference between intervention and interference. Coaches coach; they don't play the game.

As I've already noted, no one can make people build social capital. But the leader-coach *can* manage the *conditions of interaction*, raising the probability that people will do so.[7] To build social capital as an organizational competence, you must take control, creating the conditions of interaction that foster the development of social capital. But also you must let go, step back, and allow people to flourish by building the personal and social networks they need.

□

■ Social Architecture and the Conditions of Interaction

What do I mean by "conditions of interaction"? Rather than describe the concept, I'll illustrate it with an example I learned
from my colleague Jerry Davis, a classic study by Leon Festinger,
Stanley Schachter, and Kurt Back.[8] This example is about the relationship between physical architecture and social networks.
As you'll see later on, physical design is a tool you can use to
promote the creation of social capital. But physical architecture
can also be thought of as a metaphor for *social architecture*—the
design of a group or organization.

Imagine it's 1946, and you're a veteran returning from
World War II. Your application to the undergraduate program
at Massachusetts Institute of Technology (MIT) has been ac-
cepted. With support from the GI Bill, you enter the program,
and you and your spouse move into married student housing at
MIT. Along with other returning veterans, you are assigned to
housing either in Westgate (100 prefabricated single-family
houses grouped into courts) or in Westgate West (17 two-story,
ten-unit apartment buildings). The site plan in Figure 5.1 shows
the physical arrangement of the two housing projects.

At the start, the hundreds of Westgate and Westgate West
residents are strangers. Who becomes friends? Using sociometric
survey techniques (ancestors of the same family of techniques
you saw in Chapter Two), the researchers found out. Later in the
academic year, they asked each resident, "What three people in
Westgate or Westgate West do you see most of socially?"[9] Now,
you might suppose that friendships develop around common
interests, similarities in background, and the like. As it turns out,
however, the accident of physical proximity explained just about
everything. From the researchers' report:

> The most striking item was the dependence of friendship for-
> mation on the mere physical arrangement of the houses. People
> who lived close to one another became friendly with each other,

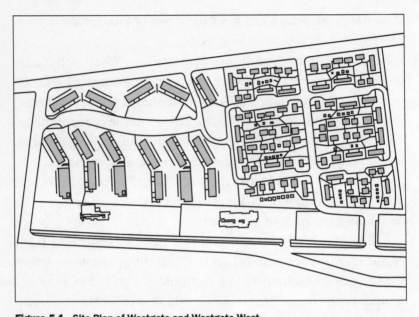

Figure 5.1. Site Plan of Westgate and Westgate West
Source: Leon Festinger, Stanley Schachter, and Kurt Back. *Social Pressures in Informal Groups: A Study of Human Factors in Housing* (Stanford, Calif.: Stanford University Press, 1950), figure 2. Used with permission.

while people who lived far apart did not. Mere "accidents" of where a path went or whose doorway a staircase passed were major determinants of who became friends within this community. The small face-to-face social groups which formed were, to a large extent, determined by the fact that a number of people lived in the same apartment building or in the same court.[10]

As discussed in Chapter Three, networks form around common activities and places. This is the principle of the "focused organization" of social networks.[11] In this case, physical proximity "focused" the veterans' social networks. In effect, proximity led to friendship. I'm sure this finding shocked the veterans. It would shock most people, because the proximity effect seems to contradict sacred precepts of freedom of choice and self-determination. When asked how they pick their friends, most people cite "shared values" or "common interests."[12] Yet the reverse is true. Your friends often *don't* share values or interests at the start. Rather, you become friends with people you happen to encounter in your communities and workplaces. "We're friends with the people we do things with," writes Malcolm Gladwell, "not necessarily with the people we resemble. We don't seek our friends; we simply associate with the people who occupy the same physical places that we do."[13]

Of course, you *are* free to choose your friends, and mere proximity is no guarantee of friendship. But none of us is free to determine the "selection set"—the collection of people you encounter *who could be your friends.* You can't become friends with people you never meet face-to-face (or virtually). Factors outside your control and even outside your awareness shape the selection set. For example, college admissions officers decide who's in and who's out. Perhaps the returning veteran who would have been your very best friend—had you had the opportunity to met him—was denied admission to MIT. You could still run into him someday, somewhere, but it's unlikely. Perhaps another friendship candidate decided to avoid married student housing, living instead in a Boston student ghetto. You're unlikely to meet him, either. If you live in Westgate, you're unlikely to run into friendship candidates living in Westgate West. You're even unlikely to encounter potential friends living down your street in Westgate. No encounter, no friendship.

The proximity effect has been documented repeatedly in the literature on both social psychology and sociology. Consider the case of marriage. Are you free to marry anyone you want? In theory, yes. But marriage choices exhibit clear patterns, too. Sociologists Peter Blau and Joseph Schwartz have shown that rates of marriage across ethnic and religious lines are a simple function of the ethnic and racial mix of local communities.[14] In homogeneous communities, the same sorts of people marry; in heterogeneous communities, different sorts marry. Why? The accident of proximity defines the selection set of eligible singles.

Residents of mixed communities encounter people from diverse demographic backgrounds. Encounter, marriage.

There's more: Proximity can shape common attitudes and interests. During the study at MIT, a tenant association was proposed. Residents didn't know what to think about it, but eventually they developed strong feelings for or against it. How did residents decide what to believe? They talked with their friends. "Within each of these small face-to-face groups, group standards had developed concerning this issue. Each group exerted strong influences on its members to conform to its standard."[15] In other words, the accident of proximity determined friendship, friendship determined who talked with whom, and members of a friendship group developed the same opinions about the tenant association. The MIT researchers explored this finding by planting and tracing false rumors about a national magazine and a radio program doing stories on tenant associations. The rumors flowed through friendship links forged by the physical architecture of the community. Thus proximity determined friendships, and friendships determined how information was shared.

Of course, physical architecture doesn't explain everything. Physical design is only one lever you can pull to manage the conditions of interaction. Nevertheless, both the MIT example and a body of evidence from many other studies[16] document the same chain: proximity → networks → common attitudes and shared information. This chain contradicts common wisdom of how the world works. Most people subscribe to a different theory and use it to explain their behavior. According to this common theory, like-minded people become friends who engage in common activities: similar values and attitudes → networks → common activities.

In part, this erroneous theory is so pervasive and so believable because the myth of individualism supports it. As I noted in Chapter One, sociologist James Coleman called individualism "a broadly perpetrated fiction in modern society." Coleman characterized it this way: "This fiction is that society consists of a set of independent individuals, each of whom acts to achieve goals that are independently arrived at, and that the functioning of the social system consists of the combination of these actions of independent individuals."[17] The MIT research is only one of a host of studies that imply that people are not independent individuals, that their goals are not independently arrived at, and that groups and organizations do not consist simply of the combination of the actions of independent individuals. As psychologist Karl Weick has said, we tend to see what we believe and not "that for which one has no beliefs."[18] The conclusion that people are not independent individuals is "hard to believe" because it contradicts deeply held beliefs about individualism. But if you accept that individualism is a fiction, you can take a fresh look at the design of your groups and organizations, learning how to use social architecture to manage the conditions of interaction in ways that enhance your social capital and the social capital of those around you.

Physical architecture, as I suggested earlier, is a metaphor for social architecture. Group design and organization design focus networks, just as physical architecture does. "Individuals whose activities are organized around the same focus," notes Scott Feld, "will tend to become interpersonally tied and form a cluster"—a clump, in my language.[19] Just as physical design focuses networks, enabling the formation of some networks and constraining the formation of others, organizational design also enables and constrains networks. Organizational design creates formal clumps, focusing networks within functions, departments, or divisions. For example, a function-centered design organizes common tasks and the people who do them into clumps called departments—Finance, Marketing, Production, Sales, and so forth. Functional departments are foci of common activities, and so networks and common ways of thinking and acting arise inside them. A multidivisional design organizes tasks and people around products or services, creating clumps called divisions.

Divisions are foci of common activities, and so networks and similar ways of thinking and behaving arise in them, too. These clumps make the organization a big world—a world full of isolated regions and islands. Over time, it gets even bigger: as organizational scholar Howard Aldrich observes, activities within departments or divisions develop more and more of an internal relevance, producing homogeneity of beliefs, inattention to information that is not shared by members of the group, and detachment from other groups and the larger environment.[20] Departments and divisions become silos or chimneys.

Fish are the last to discover water. Whether one sees it or not, every organization has a social architecture that sets the conditions of interaction. Usually, people take the design of an organization for granted; they simply accept it "as is" without thinking too much about it. If you take it for granted, then you are at the mercy of unseen forces that shape and constrain the conditions of interaction within it. You cannot escape social architecture. Your only choice is whether you will take control of social architecture or let it control you. The big world of an organization becomes small when linchpins bridge clumps. The architect's job is to manage clumps and linchpins, arranging the physical and social architecture to break barriers and unite the organization.

■ Managing the Conditions of Interaction

There are countless ways, big and small, to manage the conditions of interaction. This section presents ten categories of interventions that shape social architecture. Whether by design or not, these influences on conditions of interaction are in force *right now* in your groups and organizations. As an architect of social capital, your job is to consider each category, analyze its current effects on conditions of interaction in your organization, and then judge how you might change it to improve the conditions of interaction. Social architecture exists at all levels of an organization. Depending on your current position, you may be able to influence some aspects of social architecture right now through your own actions and others only indirectly—for example, through advocacy. Regardless of your sphere of responsibility, seek first the small wins—easy changes producing positive effects on networks. Keep in mind the following three principles:

- *Principle 1. Focus on the focus.* Networks emerge around a focus of activities. You manage conditions of interaction by changing the focus of activities. By focusing on the focus, you can see how the current organization of work funnels and channels networks. You then can consider if you should retain the current focus, strengthen it, break it up, or replace it. For example, the University of Michigan Business School is departmentalized by field: finance, marketing, organizational behavior, accounting, statistics, communications, and so on. Departments focus networks: members of a department spend most of their time with each other, not with faculty from other departments. To encourage interaction across departments as well as provide an integrated learning experience for students, we created the MAP—for "multidisciplinary action projects"—program at the Business School. Each year, over four hundred MBA students are organized into MAP teams of five to six students. Each team spends seven weeks working with a business client to analyze and solve a multidisciplinary problem. Multidisciplinary faculty teams, composed of professors from different departments, supervise student teams. Thus MAP refocuses faculty activities, building networks across departmental boundaries.

- *Principle 2. Encourage entrepreneurial networks.* The goal is to change the focus of activities so that people can easily and naturally build entrepreneurial networks. But entrepreneurial networks are not a cure-all. Sometimes the right prescription calls for a tightly knit, closed network of people dedicated to a tough task. Encourage entrepreneurial networks but don't force them inappropriately.

▪ *Principle 3. Use the union strategy.* You know from Chapter Four that a network full of structural holes—an entrepreneurial network—presents two options: fill the hole (union strategy) or leave it open (disunion strategy). Filling the hole invests in the power of reciprocity. But that doesn't mean you should always fill holes; sometimes the better part of valor is leaving two people unconnected. For example, internal auditors are better able to monitor compliance with laws and accounting principles if they are independent and not personally connected with those whom they audit. Generally, however, the union strategy is the prescription for long-run success. Therefore, make architectural changes that encourage the union strategy and discourage the disunion strategy. With the union strategy as your modus operandi, you foster a culture of cooperation, trust, and mutual aid, and you invest in and invoke the power of reciprocity.

▪

Here are the ten interventions:

#1. Facility design and location. The MIT student housing study illustrates the funneling effects of physical design. Most physical designs similarly focus networks inward. But form follows function: architects design facilities to reflect and represent organization design. The Sears Tower in Chicago, now abandoned by the retail giant, was more than a symbol of hierarchy; the tower itself made it difficult to interact across organizational levels. As Sears tried to encourage networking across levels, the vertical structure was a physical barrier people couldn't overcome. A big reason why Sears moved into a new facility based on a horizontal campus design was to make it easier to interact across formal boundaries.

When physical design reinforces functional barriers, the results can be disastrous. Before it was reorganized and privatized in 1998, the Brazilian telecommunications utility, then called Telebras, operated as a strict functional organization, divided into three broad areas: Commercial, Operations, and Administration. Eric Monteiro, a management consultant, observed that physical separation reinforced the functional chasm: Operations was located in a separate building, seldom interacting with the other functions. Not surprisingly, Operations made investment and expansion decisions without input from the Commercial Department. Some sectors, such as small towns, were overserved, while others were grossly underserved. Consumers in the major cities of São Paulo and Rio de Janeiro, for example, were forced to pay $4,000 to $5,000 on the black market to get a phone line!

The Japanese have long recognized the effect of physical design on networks, opting to use open office designs to manage the conditions of interaction. As Aundrea Almond-Wallace describes, based on her experiences working in Japan:

In most Japanese offices, there are no cubicles for employees, and there are few walled offices for managers. Hierarchy is demonstrated through one's proximity to the window. Members of the same group (functional or product-related) sit in a row of desks which are lined up perpendicular to the window. Phones are shared among employees. The manager of the cluster sits at a desk at the end of the row, closest to the window, and the manager for the whole department has a desk a bit separated from the rows of desks, even closer to the window. He manages three "clusters" who are lined up parallel to each other. The close proximity of colleagues, as well as the common phone lines, promotes close communication among members of the same cluster. There is also a lot of communication between parallel clusters within the same functional or product group.[21]

Capital Partners, a commercial real estate development firm, constructed an open office design right from the start. There are no private offices, cubicles, or physical barriers of any sort. The CEO's "office" is a desk in a corner of the open facility. This layout promotes easy interaction and frequent communication. As a leasing agent told me, "You are always overhearing conversations. You can't help it. And then you are brought into the deal."[22] Open-office layouts are the trend, according to research conducted by Steelcase, a leading designer of workplace environments. The Steelcase Web site contains good ideas, facts, and examples (http://www.steelcase.com).

The most exciting case I know of is the novel research environment at the Institute of Cancer and Developmental Biology in Cambridge (England). As Alun Anderson describes in *Science*, the Institute boosts scientific creativity by using physical architecture to enable networks:

> In its physical design—laid out by scientists for scientists—the institute is unique. Corridors circle around, vanishing abruptly in open-plan laboratories. The idea is not simply to save space but to maximize chance encounters, forcing researchers to pass through other laboratories to get to their own. The point: The researchers behind this lab believe that critical conversation and chance encounters are the lifeblood of scientific creativity. . . . There is no library; journals, after all, can be passed along and provide yet other opportunities for interaction. But there is a central facility that all the researchers agree is extremely important—a sunny and spacious tea room. There everyone, regardless of interests, is expected to mingle.[23]

You may not have the luxury of designing a complete facility from scratch, like Capital Partners, Sears, or the British Institute, but there are things you can do. It can be as simple as knocking down non–load bearing walls, rearranging office furniture, chucking out cubicle walls and dividers, relocating separate groups on one floor or in a single room, or renting temporary space.

#2. Hiring. Most hiring decisions are based on human capital: what the candidate knows. Building social capital as an organizational competence means hiring on the basis of networks as well: *who* the candidate knows, along with the candidate's ability and appetite for building networks.

Networks are so obviously important in some industries that employers know they must take a candidate's social capital into account. For example, Private Client Services, an investment bank department catering to wealthy individuals, asks job candidates about community involvement, board and club memberships, hometown connections, and so on. "They are interested in the social and business networks of their new hires," Chris Workman told me after interviewing with several investment banks. Insurance is another industry where personal and business networks obviously matter. Insurance companies use personality tests to measure social capital, but (as noted in Chapter Two) personality doesn't necessarily correlate with social capital. Sociometric methods such as those used in that chapter are more valid.

People in other businesses can learn from these two examples. The fact is that networks matter in all industries, all businesses, all organizations. Take into account the type of networks required for the job, and then assess the quality of each candidate's social capital. Even without sociometric tools, you can get a sense of a candidate's social capital by looking at a résumé through your network lens: Is the candidate an active member of various associations, boards, and outside groups? Has the candidate held positions requiring good networks? Has the candidate rotated jobs and positions, building ties along the way? Probe candidates' history of relationships in previous jobs, such as the connections they formed outside their immediate functional area, what social functions they were a part of within the organization, and so forth.

#3. Multidisciplinary teams. It's hard to find a management consultant or organizational scholar who doesn't laud the use of multidisciplinary or cross-functional teams, and for good reason. Teams are now the "basic building block of the new architecture."[24] This building block replaces the old building material, the function. Teams focus networks, just as functions do. But instead of focusing networks inside a single function, they focus networks across functions. Teams are natural bridge-building foci of activities; teams implement the union strategy.

What is a team? A team is more than a group or collection of individuals. "A team is a small number of people with complementary skills who are committed to a common purpose, performance goals, and approach for which they hold themselves mutually accountable."[25] This definition from *The Wisdom of Teams* by Jon Katzenbach and Douglas Smith contains all the right ingredients. Each ingredient is necessary; each contributes to a common focus of attention and activities that builds strong networks across areas of expertise and knowledge.

#4. Rotation programs. Formal job rotations are time-honored practices. Traditionally, these programs were used for training new management hires, or developing management talent over time as part of formal career and succession planning programs.[26] The advantages include the natural creation of entrepreneurial networks, cross-fertilization of ideas, knowledge transfer across formal boundaries, and development of a broad, multidisciplinary perspective. Today, however, orderly job rotations are giving way to a much less productive approach, which organizational scholars Nancy Tennant Snyder and Deborah Duarte call *chaotic role movements:* "the rapid movement of professionals and managers into new roles within a company in which the number of roles exceed the number of qualified people available."[27] The results are disastrous, they note, including "loss of organizational memory, lack of continuity in assignments, lack of follow-through on projects, and the continual re-

learning of best practices."[28] Their prescription is to analyze the extent of chaotic role movements in your organization; if you find that role movements are so rapid and disorderly that you are losing the benefits of job rotation, you may have to institute policies and programs to control the rate and pattern of job movements.

#5. Education. Building and using social capital require behavior and attitude changes. Education programs are key places for people to learn about, observe, explore, and practice new behaviors. GE's vaunted Crotonville management education center in New York is probably the best known; it plays a central role in CEO Jack Welch's strategy to continuously improve this giant organization.[29] He visits Crotonville twice a month, speaking with and teaching more than a thousand GE executives and managers each year.[30] But many leaders have recognized the value of education. The number of corporate universities has grown over the past decade from a few hundred to over two thousand. Further, custom programs, where faculty of a business school design and deliver sessions for a single company, are the fastest-growing segment of executive education programs.[31]

Building social capital as an organizational competence means providing significant, regular opportunities for training on building entrepreneurial networks and using social capital. You can choose from a variety of delivery options and learning models. Inside training is important, but outside may be even more important, because it provides natural opportunities to build external ties. Establish training budgets and schedules. Education should be included in everyone's annual plan and commitments, and no one should be exempt—not even the CEO. For example, CEO Thomas Caprel (whom you met in Chapter Two) includes two professional advisers in his core network. He makes lifelong learning a routine.

The range and number of educational opportunities are enormous. Consider executive education programs at top business schools and the services of training companies. Many associations sponsor training programs, as well as providing opportunities for informal coaching, mentoring, and peer support. Tom Caprel, for example, regularly attends talks, seminars, and educational programs offered by his associations.

The first step to taking advantage of education, write my University of Michigan Business School colleagues Brian Talbot, associate dean of executive education, and Joe White, dean, is simple but profound: Recognize that education is a powerful tool and use it.[32]

#6. Communities of practice. The original communities of practice, as described in Chapter Three, arose outside official channels to solve problems the organization did not equip technicians to handle. Company training and documentation were poor resources for figuring out how to solve complex technical problems. So the frustrated service technicians built informal networks to gain access to a missing resource—their collective knowledge of the problems they encountered.[33] You shouldn't wait for these communities to arise spontaneously. Allocate company resources to encourage and officially support communities of practice, using firms like Ford Motor Company as role models of best practices. A thriving community of practice needs a mechanism for communicating, linking problems and solutions, sharing and storing knowledge, and organizational learning.[34] Members should be given the time they need to participate in the community. Of course, a community of practice should have an explicit business purpose and a set of performance goals, and should be held accountable.

#7. Participatory processes. You have some tools at your disposal that may not appear at first to be ways to build social capital as an organizational competence. The formal budgeting process is one example, as accounting professor Noah Barsky and his colleagues describe.[35] Traditionally, annual rites of corporate budgeting are a top-down affair: top managers dictate

performance targets and allocate resources. But corporate budgeting can be configured as a bottom-up participatory process, involving managers from all levels and all functions. A participatory process can "eliminate hierarchy and better integrate the network of managers."[36] But it achieves these objectives only if the finance function transfers control and influence to frontline managers. This requires a fundamental mind shift, from the role of finance as corporate police to business advocate. Examples outside of finance that can be configured as network-building participatory processes include continuous improvement and quality initiatives, educational programs (if employees become teacher-facilitators in the process), and organizational redesign efforts.

#8. Management networks. A management network is a coterie of managers that transcends formal boundaries. "The members," says Ram Charan, "are drawn from across the company's functions, business units, and geography, and from different levels in the hierarchy."[37] These networks are used in companies as diverse as GE, Royal Bank of Canada, AT&T, and Conrail. For example, Jack Welch created GE's well-known Corporate Executive Council in 1986, and it has been running since.[38] Its members are the top twenty-five to thirty executives from around the company, who meet every three months to exchange ideas, share information, learn about problems, spread good practices, and provide each other with moral support. This is a high-level example in a giant company, but management networks are beneficial at almost any level in virtually any size organization in any industry—anywhere people are separated by distance or organizational or cultural boundaries.

These examples represent the applicability of the concept of management networks in diverse settings. Former New York Police Department Deputy Commissioner Jack Maple doesn't call his innovation—named Comstat—a management network but that's what it is.[39] Comstat is a weekly meeting of precinct, narcotics, and squad commanders; it is a live audit of police performance, designed to fight crime by breaking down the "blue wall of silence" between police functions. In manufacturing, one of my clients, which has about three thousand employees organized into four major divisions, holds a monthly meeting of the divisional presidents. They get together without an audience, to share ideas and information and build trust in the process. When they skip meetings, tensions and distrust rise. (This is the group mentioned in Chapter Four, where one of the presidents told the others that he found himself starting to lose confidence in them if the meetings weren't held often enough.) Another client, real estate firm Capital Partners, has only 150 employees but they are spread across three counties and three markets—commercial, retail, and industrial real estate development. Its senior partners operate as a management network, meeting regularly to knit together their operations.

#9. External networks. External networks link the interior life of an organization with its environment. These networks break the boundaries between an organization and its customers and suppliers. Without these networks, all sorts of problems arise. There are countless examples, but consider an unusual one to emphasize the point: NASA and its error-riddled Mars exploration program. A NASA investigation into the September 1999 loss of the $125 million spacecraft, the *Mars Climate Orbiter*, revealed that a contributing cause was lack of communication across organizational boundaries: "Questions about the orbiter's trajectory raised by navigators were not relayed to other groups within the project, including the spacecraft's builders at Lockheed Martin Astronautics in Colorado."[40]

The foci of external networks include customer relationships, supplier partnerships, alliances with competitors, and board memberships. A wide variety of structures and mechanisms are used. For example, some companies reorganize into customer-focused teams, each concentrated on a single customer or a small group of customers. Others focus on building alliances with competitors—Corning, for example, has transformed its organizational design into a network of alliances. Some companies create a formal role, the alliance manager, to oversee a network of alliances; British Petroleum created a committee for this purpose.[41] Yet other companies create what I call association support systems to help their executives find and serve on outside association boards of directors. Arthur Andersen is an example. The accounting giant actually requires that its partners join boards.

#10. Incentive systems. Many companies ask for behaviors they don't reward. Steve Kerr calls this "the folly of rewarding A, while hoping for B."[42] For example, many financial services companies exhort their salespeople to "cross-market" but don't financially reward people who share leads and make sales as a team. Collective rewards encourage building and using social capital; individual rewards are barriers to social capital. Recall the network dilemma posed in Chapter Four. If this scenario took place in a company with an incentive system based on individual performance and immediate financial gain, the union strategy would be a tough choice. One would have to make the sale and lose the long-term investment in social capital.

If you are hoping for people to make decisions that build long-term social capital, then you have to reward these behaviors. This means some combination of individual and collective incentives. Consider the hybrid system Jerre Stead established when he was chair and CEO of AT&T Global Information Solutions (the old NCR Corporation). He called it the 1 over 1 system, where 50 percent of a person's compensation is based on individual performance and 50 percent on collective performance—by a team, group, division, or some other meaningful unit with which the person was involved. The 1 over 1 system was used for *everyone* at the company. Of course, there is no such thing as a perfect incentive system. Every system has defects that are revealed only as the system runs. GE's sunset provision for new incentive systems is the best alternative to perfection: any new incentive system automatically ceases operation after twelve months. This provision allows defects to be corrected and makes sure an incentive system doesn't become immortal.

After years of research and consulting on networks, I've concluded that the incentive system is the single biggest obstacle to building social capital. But my conclusion doesn't mean that changing *just* the incentive system is enough. Piling on pressure to perform without providing the tools to perform leads to frustration, not better results. Sometimes it leads to unethical or illegal behavior. For example, unrealistic revenue targets emphasizing "sales at all costs" can drive managers to conspire with their competitors, fixing prices and rigging market shares, unless the company also invests in research to invent new products or engineering to improve old ones.[43] Fierce pressures on New York City teachers and administrators to raise standardized test scores appear to have produced the massive cheating alleged in a December 1999 report. According to investigators, teachers allegedly gave out questions in advance, pointed out incorrect answers, and even completed test forms for students.[44] My interpretation is that the incentives to raise scores weren't matched with new tools and additional resources to improve learning.

■ Conclusion: Building the Network Organization

Implementing any of these ten categories of interventions will help you establish building social capital as an organizational competence. To maximize their effects, however, they should be considered as the parts that make a whole: the network organization. This organizational design goes by other names, such as the seamless enterprise or the boundaryless organization. I prefer to call the design by what it is—a network—rather than by what it lacks—an organization without seams or boundaries. No matter the name, the architectural design is the same: as I have defined it, the network organization is "a social network that is *integrated* across formal boundaries. Interpersonal ties of any type are formed without respect to formal groups or categories."[45] Examples include GE's boundaryless organization, Corning's network of alliances, and the commercial real estate firm Capital Partners. A unit of a company can adopt the network organization design, building social capital as an organizational competence by using the interventions described in this chapter. The Pharmaceutical Research Institute at Bristol-Myers Squibb is an excellent role model.

Building Social Capital

Bristol-Myers Squibb's Pharmaceutical Research Institute (PRI) is transforming itself to compete in the new millennium, building social capital to boost its ability to identify, develop, and commercialize blockbuster drugs.

You may know Bristol-Myers Squibb for its personal care products such as Clairol and Excedrin, but over 70 percent of its $20 billion annual sales comes from pharmaceuticals, including cardiovascular treatments, cholesterol-reduction drugs, anticancer drugs, and anti-infective drugs. Innovative new drugs are essential to Bristol-Myers Squibb's continuing success and growth, and therefore, PRI plays center stage in the company.

PRI has already produced a number of blockbuster products, so why change a winning formula? After conducting a comprehensive strategic analysis, PRI leaders concluded that the Institute had to make a series of process, organizational, and leadership changes to thrive in a dramatically changing world of health care. "We looked at changes likely to occur in the external environment that would impact the pharmaceutical industry and its ability to develop new medicines," says PRI's president, Dr. Peter S. Ringrose. These changes include new technologies such as genomics and informatics as well as societal factors such as better-informed consumers, an aging population, and the potential of more government intervention and control.

The PRI leadership also analyzed their most successful and rapidly growing competitors. They learned that "having a number of blockbuster products was a strong determinant of success and ability to grow in the marketplace," says Dr. Ringrose. "There's a clear correlation between the ability to create innovative blockbusters and the ability to grow and to move into new areas of therapeutic opportunity."

PRI decided to sharpen its strategy, focusing on Opportunity-Seeking Blockbusters, or OSBs. "A blockbuster," Dr. Ringrose says, "is a product that generates global sales in excess of one billion dollars per year." PRI's goal is three blockbuster drugs per year by 2003, with even more blockbusters per year after that.

To implement OSB and achieve its ambitious goals, Dr. Ringrose adds, "We must create an entrepreneurial culture that encourages innovation and flexibility, that fosters speed in testing new hypotheses, and enhances greater networking both internally and externally. As you break down the walls, the networking and flow of information increases. People become more comfortable sharing knowledge, and the whole social capital and productivity of the organization increases."

PRI's transformation includes a number of organizational and cultural changes:

- *Process-based architectural blueprint.* PRI, like many R&D groups, had been a traditional departmentalized organization. The new OSB design encompasses the processes that advance an idea from inception to commercial success. As Dr. Ringrose explains, "We wanted to break though the traditional silos of the functional departments and create a seamless flow from the point of molecular concept to the launch of a novel product into the marketplace. This means getting a new alignment between the functions—organic chemistry, pharmacology, molecular biology, clinical medicine, biostatistics, computer sciences—and the process by which we conduct research and development in the modern pharmaceutical industry. We wanted to turn the organizational architecture on its side and focus on the process."

- *Process-oriented governance structure.* PRI has created a governance structure aligned with the process of taking a new idea to full commercialization. There are now four Operating Committees: Lead Discovery, Exploratory Development, Full Development, and Licensing Management.

- *Dual roles and reporting responsibilities.* Each Operating Committee has co-chairs, bridging functional and process responsibilities. Senior managers also have dual roles. "We made a conscious decision to blur the areas of responsibility and to ensure that we got buy-in from the supporting functions," says Dr. Ringrose. "A number of co-chairs have dual functional and process responsibilities. We created dual responsibility for most of the senior management. I see their process roles and functional roles as equally important."

- *Common goals.* The OSB strategy galvanized the organization behind a common goal. "It was the first time that some parts of the organization really understood what we were after," acknowledges Dr. Ringrose. "It delivered a very clear message."

- *Multidisciplinary teams.* Multidisciplinary teams are formed around pharmaceutical compounds with blockbuster potential. Each team leader has the responsibility for moving the compound through the entire development process. By design, the team leaders have little line responsibility for the support functions within their project groups. "Their challenge is to find new ways of making the network work," Dr. Ringrose says. "Given all the different scientific disciplines, the key to success is having multidisciplinary teams and networks, in addition to cross-functional groups that support the different parts of the processes."

- *Rotations.* Distance and geography are barriers to networking. Because the PRI conducts clinical studies all over the world, it needs to overcome the barrier of distance. "We may move people between different functions and geographies so they spend real time working in other locations or other functional or process groups," notes Dr. Ringrose. "We are consciously managing this cross-fertilization, rather than leaving it to Brownian motion."

- *Rewards and incentives.* The PRI has established a new system of rewards and recognition. Metrics are utilized at all stages of the R&D

process, from early discovery, lead optimization, and exploratory development to full development. The new system aims to reward entrepreneurial behavior and innovation at all stages of the process.

- *Formal and informal meetings across levels and groups.* Networks are built across levels and groups via formal and informal meetings. These include Town Hall style meetings, Summit Meetings between the commercial and scientific sides, informal lunches across functions, and Dr. Ringrose's regular informal meetings with staff at all levels from around the organization.

- *Learning organization.* The PRI has institutionalized the concept of a learning organization. As Dr. Ringrose explains, "When we reach a goal, such as a clinical proof of principle or a regulatory approval, we review what we learned from the exercise and share our conclusions and observations. Whether the outcome was a success or failure, we share knowledge across all the other groups," he says.

How well has the OSB transformation worked? PRI is still undergoing its transition to a process-driven organization, and Dr. Ringrose calls it "an experiment in progress." Yet the PRI has already benefited from significant cultural changes, new behaviors, and the discovery and development of new drugs with blockbuster potential.

"The whole organization is energized," reports Dr. Ringrose. "This energization enables new concepts to be introduced, such as the importance of networking, and helps us reinforce themes, such as social capital."

"A pleasant surprise," he says, "was that by redefining functions and renaming groups, we unleashed a lot of cooperation and creativity. The light came on in people's minds that doing things differently was actually allowed and indeed encouraged."

An excellent example of the new cooperative spirit was PRI's portfolio evaluation process. "Picking the winners is the mantra of this process," says Dr. Ringrose. "Coming to that decision in a crisp way is a challenge. Last year, for the first time, various groups across the organization readily agreed to engage in this debate. About thirty senior managers from R&D and the business spent two days together. "The participants wrestled with a perennial problem," Dr. Ringrose explained. "Where should PRI best invest its resources? What projects and compounds should it fund, and which should it drop? You couldn't tell who was from R&D and who was from the commercial side, because both sides were considering choices from the perspective of the other. This debate allowed us to make better decisions about resource allocation. Today when you walk into a meeting of the multifunctional global brand teams, it's hard to distinguish the scientists from the marketers."

Of course, the proof of the pudding is in the tasting. "The ultimate measure of success," notes Dr. Ringrose, "will be achieving the goal of OSB in the marketplace." The new PRI already has several new drugs with blockbuster potential in the pipeline.

Source: Company materials and interview with Dr. Peter S. Ringrose.

The goal of building social capital as an organizational competence is the same as building it as an individual competence—to increase the ability to achieve goals, fulfill missions, and make positive contributions to the world. As an individual, you can control your own fate by building social capital, whether or not the organization supports you. And as an architect of the network organizational design, you can magnify the power of individuals many times over by building social capital as an organizational competence, orchestrating human activities in service to others.

CHAPTER SUMMARY

This chapter moved the discussion of social capital from the individual to the organizational level. Trends and changes in the business world make building social capital as an organizational competence more important than ever before. This competence looks for the source of sustained success in the right place—human culture and human capabilities. Good leaders, no matter where they are in the organization, are good social architects. They take control of the organization, making deep changes in conditions of interaction, and then stand back to allow networks to blossom, thrive, and flourish.

Physical design is a tool for managing social networks, and also a metaphor for social architecture—the design of a group or organization. Physical proximity strongly influences relationships, attitudes, and behaviors, and social architecture has the same effects. It shapes networks by controlling the focus of human activities. By changing the focus, you change networks.

Useful interventions can be described in ten categories: facility design and location, hiring, multidisciplinary teams, rotation programs, education, communities of practice, management networks, external networks, and incentive systems. Each intervention builds social capital, but together they produce a state change: the network organization. This design is the blueprint for social capital architecture. By implementing it, the organization of human activities is focused on building and using social capital in service to others.

Notes

Preface

1. Edward M. Hallowell, *Connect: Twelve Vital Ties That Open Your Heart, Lengthen Your Life, and Deepen Your Soul* (New York: Pantheon Books, 1999).
2. Documented in Robert E. Quinn, Regina M. O'Neill, and Lynda St. Clair (eds.), *Pressing Problems in Modern Organizations* (New York: AMACOM, 2000).

Chapter One

1. James S. Coleman, *Foundations of Social Theory* (Cambridge, Mass.: Harvard University Press, 1990), p. 300.
2. Jeffery Pfeffer also makes this point on pp. 17–18 in *Managing with Power* (Cambridge, Mass.: Harvard Business School Press, 1992).
3. This is the classic nature/nurture debate. For the role of the environment in shaping "intelligence," broadly defined, see for example, chapter 2 in Robert J. Sternberg, *Successful Intelligence: How Practical and Creative Intelligence Determine Success in Life* (New York: Penguin Books, 1997), and chapter 12 in Daniel Goleman, *Emotional Intelligence* (New York: Bantam Books, 1997).
4. Sternberg, *Successful Intelligence*, pp. 85–86. See also D. K. Detterman and Robert J. Sternberg (eds.), *How and How Much Can Intelligence*

Be Increased? (Norwood, N.J.: Ablex, 1982). On the trend of rising IQ scores around the world, see James R. Flynn, "Massive IQ Gains in Fourteen Nations: What IQ Tests Really Measure," *Psychological Bulletin* 101 (1987): 171–191; Ulric Neisser (ed.), *The Rising Curve: Long-Term Gains in IQ and Related Measures* (American Psychological Association, 1998).

5. I. Lazer and R. Darlington, "Lasting Effects of Early Education: A Report from the Consortium for Longitudinal Studies," *Monographs of the Society for Research in Child Development* 47 (1982); E. Zigler and W. Berman, "Discerning the Future of Early Childhood Intervention," *American Psychologist* 38 (1983): 894–906. Sternberg cites and discusses these studies in chapter 2 of *Successful Intelligence.*

6. See Sternberg's summary and discussion of a variety of empirical studies that make these points, *Successful Intelligence,* pp. 86–87.

7. Leslie Brothers, *Friday's Footprint: How Society Shapes the Human Mind* (Oxford, England: Oxford University Press, 1997). On emotion as relationship, see, for example, chapter 9 in Kenneth J. Gergen, *Realities and Relationships* (Cambridge, Mass.: Harvard University Press, 1994).

8. Brothers, *Friday's Footprint,* p. xii.

9. Thomas Lewis, Fari Amini, and Richard Lannon, *A General Theory of Love* (New York: Random House, 2000).

10. James S. Coleman, "Social Capital in the Creation of Human Capital," *American Journal of Sociology* 94 (1988): S95-S120.

11. Robert K. Merton, *Social Theory and Social Structure* (New York: Free Press, 1968).

12. Richard Swedberg, *Max Weber and the Idea of Economic Sociology* (Princeton: Princeton University Press, 1998). Note that Islamic law today forbids charging interest on a loan, speculating in precious metals, and investing in "sin" industries, among other prohibitions. Recently, Dow Jones created its Islamic Market Index, which includes companies that conform to Islamic principles.

13. Max Gunther, *The Luck Factor* (New York: Macmillan, 1977).

14. Chapter 6, "Managing Serendipity," in Wayne E. Baker, *Networking Smart: How to Build Relationships for Personal and Organizational Success* (New York: McGraw-Hill, 1994).

15. For example, see Paul Adler and Seok-Woo Kwon, "Social Capital: The Good, the Bad, and the Ugly," working paper, University of California, Los Angeles, Business School, 1999; Baker, *Networking Smart*; Roger Th. A. J. Leenders and Shaul M. Gabbay (eds.), *Corporate Social Capital and Liability* (Norwell, Mass.: Kluwer, 1999), chapter 4; Ronald S. Burt, *Structural Holes: The Social Structure of Competition* (Cambridge, Mass.: Harvard University Press, 1992); Ronald S. Burt, "The Social Capital of Entrepreneurial Managers," *Financial Times* (European Edition, May 10, 1996); Ronald S. Burt, "The Network Structure of Social Capital," in Robert I. Sutton and Barry M. Staw (eds.), *Research in Organizational Behavior* (Greenwich, Conn.: JAI Press, 2000); Coleman, "Social Capital in the Creation of Human Capital," Jane E. Fountain, "Social Capital: Its Relationship to Innovation in Science and Technology," *Science and Public Policy* 25 (1998): 103–155; Jane Jacobs, *The Death and Life of Great American Cities* (New York: Penguin Books, 1965); Nan Lin, "Building a Network Theory of Social Capital," *Connections* 22 (1999): 28–51; Janine Nahapiet and Sumantra Ghoshal, "Social Capital, Intellectual Capital, and the Organizational Advantage," *Academy of Management Review* 23 (1998): 242–266; Pamela Paxton, "Is Social Capital Declining in the United States? A Multiple Indicator Assessment," *American Journal of Sociology* 105 (1999): 88–127; Joel M. Podolny and James Baron, "Resources and Relationships: Social Networks and Mobility in the Workplace," *American Sociological Review* 62 (1997): 673–693; Robert D. Putnam, *Making Democracy Work* (Princeton, N.J.: Princeton University Press, 1993); Robert D. Putnam, *Bowling Alone: The Collapse and Revival of American Community* (New York: Simon & Schuster, 2000). G. Walker, B. Kogut, and W. Shan, "Social Capital, Structural Holes, and the Formation of an Industrial Network," *Organization Science* 8 (1997): 109–125.

16. For example, see Roberto M. Fernandez and N. Weinberg, "Sifting and Sorting: Personal Contacts and Hiring in a Retail Bank," *American Sociological Review* 62 (1997): 883–902.

17. Mark Granovetter, *Getting a Job* (Cambridge, Mass.: Harvard University Press, 1973).

18. For example, see Ed A.W. Boxman, Paul M. De Graaf, and Hendrick D. Flap, "The Impact of Social and Human Capital on the Income Attainment of Dutch Managers," *Social Networks* 13 (1991): 51–73; H. Flap and E. Boxman, "Getting a Job as a Manager," in Leenders and Gabbay (eds.), *Corporate Social Capital and Liability,* chapter 11; Rebecca Sandefur, Edward O. Laumann, and John P. Heinz, "The Changing Value of Social Capital in an Expanding Social System: Lawyers in the Chicago Bar, 1975 and 1995," in Leenders and Gabbay (eds.), *Corporate Social Capital and Liability,* chapter 12.

19. Burt, *Structural Holes;* Burt, "The Social Capital of Entrepreneurial Managers"; Burt, "The Network Structure of Social Capital."

20. The classic statement is John R. P. French Jr. and Bertram Raven, "The Bases of Social Power," in *Group Dynamics,* 3rd ed., edited by Dorwin Cartwright and Alvin Zander (New York: Harper & Row, 1968), pp. 259–269. For an update and elaboration, see Part II in Pfeffer, *Managing with Power.* For an empirical test, see Noah E. Friedkin, "Structural Bases of Interpersonal Influence in Groups: A Longitudinal Case Study," *American Sociological Review* 58 (1993): 861–872.

21. Baker, *Networking Smart*; Aimee Arlington and Wayne E. Baker, "Serving Two (or More) Masters: The Challenge and Promise of Multiple Accountabilities," in *Pressing Problems in Modern Organizations,* edited by Robert E. Quinn, Regina M. O'Neill, and Lynda St. Clair (New York: AMACOM, 2000), chapter 2.

22. Linda A. Hill, *Becoming a Manager* (Cambridge, Mass.: Harvard Business School Press, 1992); John J. Gabarro, *The Dynamics of Taking Charge* (Cambridge, Mass.: Harvard Business School Press, 1987).

23. Pfeffer, *Managing with Power,* discusses results from various studies; see pp. 112–116.

24. David Krackhardt, "Cognitive Social Structures," *Social Networks* 9 (1987): 109–134; David Krackhardt, "Assessing the Political Landscape: Structure, Cognition and Power in Organizations," *Administrative Science Quarterly* 35 (1990): 342–369.

25. For example, see Robert J. Gaston and Sharon Bell, "The Informal Supply of Capital," final report submitted to the U.S. Small Business Administration by the Applied Economics Group, 1988. See also W. D. Bygrave, "Syndicated Investments by Venture Capital Firms: A

Networking Perspective," *Journal of Business Venturing* 2 (1987): 139–154; J. O. Fiet, "Reliance Upon Informants in the Venture Capital Industry," *Journal of Business Venturing* 10 (1995): 195–223.

26. Brian Uzzi, "Embeddedness in the Making of Financial Capital: How Social Relations and Networks Benefit Firms Seeking Financing," *American Sociological Review* 64 (1999): 481–505; Brian Uzzi and James J. Gillespie, "Corporate Social Capital and the Cost of Financial Capital: An Embeddedness Approach," in Leenders and Gabbay (eds.), *Corporate Social Capital and Liability,* chapter 24; Wayne E. Baker, "Market Networks and Corporate Behavior," *American Journal of Sociology* 96 (1990): 589–625.

27. Robert J. Shiller and John Pound, "Survey Evidence of Diffusion of Interest and Information Among Investors," *Journal of Economic Behavior and Organization* 12 (1989): 47–66; Robert Shiller, *Market Volatility* (Cambridge, Mass.: MIT Press, 1991).

28. Wayne E. Baker, "The Social Structure of a National Securities Market," *American Journal of Sociology* 89 (1984): 775–811; "Floor Trading and Crowd Dynamics," in *The Social Dynamics of Financial Markets* (Greenwich, Conn.: JAI Press, 1984); Wayne E. Baker and Ananth Iyer, "Information Networks and Market Behavior," *Journal of Mathematical Sociology* 16 (1992): 305–332.

29. Jeffrey Pfeffer and Robert I. Sutton, *The Knowing-Doing Gap* (Boston: Harvard Business School Press, 2000), p. 18. On the knowledge society, see, for example, Carl Shapiro and Hal R. Varian, *Information Rules* (Boston: Harvard Business School Press, 1999).

30. "The Real Meaning of On-the-Job Training." *Leader to Leader* (Fall 1998): 61. Cited and discussed on p. 18 in Pfeffer and Sutton, *The Knowing-Doing Gap.*

31. Summarized in chapter 8 of Pfeffer and Sutton, *The Knowing-Doing Gap.*

32. Baker, *Networking Smart,* chapter 11.

33. Everett M. Rogers, *Diffusion of Innovations,* 4th ed. (New York: Free Press, 1995).

34. Toby E. Stuart, "Technological Prestige and the Accumulation of Alliance Capital," in Leenders and Gabbay (eds.), *Corporate Social Capital and Liability,* chapter 20.

35. Ranjay Gulati, "Social Structure and Alliance Formation Patterns: A Longitudinal Analysis," *Administrative Science Quarterly* 40 (1995): 619–652.

36. Richard A. D'Aveni and Idalene F. Kesner, "Top Managerial Prestige, Power, and Tender Offer Response: A Study of Elite Social Networks and Target Firm Cooperation During Takeovers," *Organization Science* 4 (1993): 123–151.

37. Gerald F. Davis, "Agents without Principles? The Spread of the Poison Pill through the Intercorporate Network," *Administrative Science Quarterly* 36 (1991): 583–613; Gerald F. Davis and Henrich R. Greve, "Corporate Elite Networks and Governance Changes in the 1980s," *American Journal of Sociology* 103 (1997): 1–37.

38. Richard A. D'Aveni, "Top Managerial Prestige and Organizational Bankruptcy," *Organization Science* 1 (1990): 121–142.

39. Putnam, *Making Democracy Work.*

40. Putnam, *Bowling Alone.*

41. See, for example, Paxton, "Is Social Capital Declining in the United States?"

42. Mihaly Csikszentmihalyi, *Flow: The Psychology of Optimal Experience* (New York: Harper & Row, 1990).

43. For example, see Jean Baker Miller and Irene Pierce Stiver, *The Healing Connection* (Boston: Beacon Press, 1997); Joyce K. Fletcher, "Relational Practice," *Journal of Management Inquiry* 7 (1998): 163–186; Joyce K. Fletcher, "Developing an Interactive Self," *Social Policy* (summer 1998): 48–51; Edward M. Hallowell, *Connect: Twelve Vital Ties That Open Your Heart, Lengthen Your Life, and Deepen Your Soul* (New York: Pantheon Books, 1999).

44. Barton J. Hirsch, "Social Networks and the Coping Process: Creating Personal Communities," in *Social Networks and Social Support,* edited by Benjamin H. Gottlieb (Thousand Oaks, Calif.: Sage, 1981), 149–170, quote from p. 169.

45. For example, see S. Cohen, W. J. Doyle, D. P. Skoner, B. S. Rabin, and G. M. Gwaltney Jr., "Social Ties and Susceptibility to the Common Cold," *Journal of the American Medical Association* 277 (June 25, 1997): 1940–1944; James S. House, Karl R. Landis, and Debra Umberson, "Social Relationships and Health," *Science* 241 (1988):

540–545; J. A. House, *Work Stress and Social Support* (Reading, Mass.: Addison-Wesley, 1981); Lewis, Amini, and Lannon, *A General Theory of Love;* S. S. Jouard and T. Landsman, *Healthy Personality: An Approach from the Viewpoint of Humanistic Psychology* (New York: Macmillan, 1980); Charles Kadushin, "Social Density and Mental Health," in *Social Structure and Network Analysis,* edited by Peter V. Marsden and Nan Lin (Thousand Oaks, Calif.: Sage, 1982), pp. 147–158; Benjamin H. Gottlieb, (ed.), *Social Networks and Social Support* (Thousand Oaks, Calif.: Sage, 1981); R. S. Lazarus, "The Health-Related Functions of Social Support," *Journal of Behavioral Medicine* 4 (1981): 381–406; S. E. Taylor and J. Brown, "Illusion and Well-Being," *Psychological Bulletin* 103 (1988): 193–210; K. A. Wallston and B. S. Wallston, "Who Is Responsible for Your Health? The Construct of 'Health Locus of Control,'" in *Social Psychology of Health and Illness,* edited by G. Saunders and J. Suls (Hillsdale, N.J.: Erlbaum, 1982), pp. 65–95.

46. Gottlieb, *Social Networks and Social Support.*

47. Research statistics reported in John M. Gottman and Nan Silver, *The Seven Principles for Making Marriage Work* (New York: Crown, 1999), pp. 4–5.

48. Lisa F. Berkman and S. Leonard Syme, "Social Networks, Host Resistance, and Mortality: A Nine-Year Follow-up Study of Alameda County Residents," *American Journal of Epidemiology* 109 (1979): 186–204; House, Landis, and Umberson, "Social Relationships and Health"; Robin M. DiMatteo and Ron Hays, "Social Support and Serious Illness," in Gottlieb, *Social Networks and Social Support,* chapter 5.

49. For example, see William J. Strawbridge, Richard D. Cohen, Sarah J. Shema, and George A. Kaplan, "Frequent Attendance at Religious Services and Mortality over Twenty-Eight Years," *American Journal of Public Health* 87 (1997): 957–961; Marc A. Musick, James S. House, and David R. Williams, "Attendance at Religious Services and Mortality in a National Sample," working paper, Survey Research Center, Institute for Social Research, University of Michigan, 1998.

50. Lisa F. Berkman and S. Leonard Syme, "Social Networks, Host Resistance, and Mortality."

51. Hallowell, *Connect,* pp. 5–6.
52. Hallowell, *Connect,* p. 6.
53. Hallowell, *Connect,* pp. 5–6.
54. Hallowell, *Connect.*
55. Wayne E. Baker, "How to Survive Downsizing," *USA Today Policy Magazine* (March 1995): 74–76.
56. Wayne E. Baker and Robert R. Faulkner, "Diffusion of Fraud in the Capital Markets," paper presented at the annual meeting of the American Society of Criminology, Toronto (November 1999).
57. See also Viktor E. Frankl, *The Will to Meaning* (New York: Meridian, 1988). Originally published 1970.
58. Barry Wellman and Keith Hampton, "Living Networked On and Offline," *Contemporary Sociology* 28 (1999): 648–654; quoted material from p. 648.

Chapter Two

1. This question was asked in the General Social Survey (GSS). The GSS, a representative survey of the American population, has been conducted annually for about twenty years. This section draws from the analysis and findings presented in Ronald S. Burt, "A Note on the General Social Survey's Ersatz Network Density Item," *Social Networks* 9 (1987): 75–85.
2. See page 83 in Burt, "A Note on the General Social Survey's Ersatz Network Density Item."
3. For the study on which this is based, and a complete list of the twenty products and services, see Harry L. Davis, Stephen J. Hoch, and E. K. Easton Ragsdale, "An Anchoring and Adjustment Model of Spousal Predictions," *Journal of Consumer Research* 13 (1986): 25–37. This study included only spousal predictions. However, a subsequent study (see Note 4) examined three kinds of predictions: spouse's preferences, peer's preferences, and the typical American consumer's preferences. This study asked about attitudes rather than products and services. The results showed that levels of (low) predictive accuracy are very similar for spouses and peers. They are even lower for predictions about the typical consumer.

4. For the study on which this is based, and a complete list of the twenty-one attitude statements, see Stephen J. Hoch, "Perceived Consensus and Predictive Accuracy: The Pros and Cons of Projection," *Journal of Personality and Social Psychology* 53 (1986): 221–234.

5. I calculated these statistics by averaging the results from four experiments reported in Davis, Hoch, and Ragsdale, "An Anchoring and Adjustment Model of Spousal Predictions." The average correlation was .2705, which yields an explained variance of 7 percent.

6. I calculated these statistics from results reported in Hoch, "Perceived Consensus and Predictive Accuracy." The correlation for spouses is .506, which yields an explained variance of 26 percent. The correlation for peers is .533, which yields an explained variance of 28 percent.

7. David Krackhardt has produced a series of studies that explore the relationship between "mental maps" (cognitive social structure) and objective maps of networks, and the correlates of the accuracy of mental maps. For an early publication in this series, see his "Cognitive Social Structures," *Social Networks* 9 (1987): 109–134. See also his "Assessing the Political Landscape: Structure, Cognition, and Power in Organizations," *Administrative Science Quarterly* 35 (1990): 342–369.

8. The Baron de Rothschild story has been recounted in several places, including Robert Cialdini, "Indirect Tactics of Image Management: Beyond Basking," in *Impression Management in the Organization*, edited by R. A. Giacalone and P. Rosenfeld (Hillsdale, N.J.: Erlbaum, 1989), 45–56; Martin Kilduff and David Krackhardt, "Bringing the Individual Back In: A Structural Analysis of the Internal Market for Reputation in Organizations," *Academy of Management Journal* 37 (1994): 87–108; quote from p. 87. Kilduff and Krackhardt find, at least in the firm they studied, that "being perceived to have a prominent peer in an organization boosted an individual's reputation as a good performer, but that actually having such a peer . . . had no effect" (p. 87).

9. For an excellent book on observation skills, see John Lofland, *Analyzing Social Settings* (Belmont, Calif.: Wadsworth, 1995). Lofland makes the distinction between "knowing about" and "knowing."

10. Stanley Wasserman and Katherine Faust, *Social Network Analysis: Methods and Applications* (Cambridge, England: Cambridge University

Press, 1994). My very brief summary of the history of the field draws from chapter 1 in their book.

11. "Emotions Mapped by New Geography," *New York Times* (April 3, 1933): 17.

12. For neural networks, see, for example, Duncan J. Watts and Steven H. Strogatz, "Collective Dynamic of 'Small-World' Networks," *Nature* 393 (June 4, 1998): 440–442. For criminal networks, see, for example, Wayne E. Baker and Robert R. Faulkner, "The Social Organization of Conspiracy: Illegal Networks in the Heavy Electrical Equipment Industry," *American Sociological Review* 58 (1993): 837–860; Wayne E. Baker and Robert R. Faulkner, "Diffusion of Fraud in the Capital Markets," paper presented at the annual meeting of the American Society of Criminology, Toronto (November 1999); Malcolm Sparrow, "The Application of Network Analysis to Criminal Intelligence," *Social Networks* 13 (1991): 251–274.

13. S. A. Boorman and R. Levitt, "Big Brother and Blockmodeling," *New York Times* (November 20, 1983): F3; S. A. Boorman and P. R. Levitt, "Blockmodels and Self-Defense," *New York Times* (November 27, 1983): F3.

14. As Barry Wellman reviews in "An Egocentric Network Tale" (*Social Networks* 15 [1993]: 423–436), the pioneers include Elizabeth Bott, George Homans, Talcott Parsons, Harrison White, Charles Tilly, Edward Laumann, Barry Wellman, Mark Granovetter, Claude Fischer, Norman Shulman, and Donald Coates.

15. For example, see Ronald S. Burt, *Structural Holes: The Social Structure of Competition* (Cambridge, Mass.: Harvard University Press (1992); Ronald S. Burt, "The Social Capital of Entrepreneurial Managers," *Financial Times* (European Edition, May 10, 1996) 166; Ronald S. Burt, "A Note on Social Capital and Network Content," *Social Networks* 19 (1997): 355–373; Ronald S. Burt, "The Network Structure of Social Capital," in Robert I. Sutton and Barry M. Staw (eds.), *Research in Organizational Behavior* (Greenwich, Conn.: JAI Press, 2000).

16. This research is published in a huge array of scientific journals, dissertations, and books. For a comprehensive survey of network measures of social capital, see Stephen Borgatti, Candace Jones, and Martin G. Everett, "Network Measures of Social Capital," *Connections*

21 (1998): 27–36. Two collections of essays focus specifically on networks and social capital in organizations. (1) N. Nohria and R. G. Eccles, eds., *Networks and Organizations: Structure, Form, and Action* (Boston: Harvard Business School Press, 1992). This volume contains nineteen chapters on networks and social capital. My chapter is "The Network Organization in Theory and Practice" (chapter 15). (2) Roger Th. A. J. Leenders and Shaul M. Gabbay, eds., *Corporate Social Capital and Liability* (Norwell, Mass.: Kluwer, 1999). My chapter (with co-author David Obstfeld) is "Social Capital by Design: Structures, Strategies, and Institutional Context" (chapter 4).

17. See, for example, the references to Burt in these endnotes. Rosabeth Moss Kanter makes an early reference to the concept of "entrepreneurial managers" who reach beyond the boundaries of their formal positions to secure information, resources, and support: "The Middle Manager as Innovator," *Harvard Business Review* (July-August 1982): 95–105. See also "the power of peers" in Wayne E. Baker, *Networking Smart: How to Build Relationships for Personal and Organizational Success* (New York: McGraw-Hill, 1994), pp. 94–97.

18. See, for example, the references to Burt in Note 15 and elsewhere in these endnotes.

19. Others have also noted that being a bridge can be a source of stress. See, for example, Burt, "The Social Capital of Entrepreneurial Managers"; Joel M. Podolny and James Baron, "Resources and Relationships: Social Networks and Mobility in the Workplace," *American Sociological Review* 62 (1997): 673–693.

20. See, for example, the references to Burt in these endnotes. For similar findings for team-level entrepreneurial networks, see, for example, Kathleen M. Sutcliffe and J. Stuart Bunderson, "Management Team Learning and Business Unit Performance," working paper, University of Michigan Business School, 1999.

21. It is customary to ignore the ego-alter links when calculating the density of an egocentric network. The maximum number of alter-alter links is $(n^2 - n) / 2$, where n is the number of alters.

22. Burt, *Structural Holes,* developed and introduced "redundancy" and related concepts and measures for describing and analyzing egocentric networks. Others have since refined or amended these measures,

such as Stephen Borgatti, "Structural Holes: Unpacking Burt's Redundancy Measures," *Connections* 1997: 35–38.

23. Burt, *Structural Holes,* developed and introduced "effective size," and related concepts and measures for describing and analyzing egocentric networks. Others have since refined or corrected his measures, such as Borgatti, "Structural Holes: Unpacking Burt's Redundancy Measures."

24. Stephanie Bailey and Peter V. Marsden, "Interpretation and Interview Context: Examining the General Social Survey Name Generator Using Cognitive Methods," *Social Networks* 21 (1999): 287–309.

25. Peter V. Marsden, "Core Discussion Networks of Americans," *American Sociological Review* 52 (1987): 122–131.

26. Danching Ruan, "The Context of the General Social Survey Discussion Networks: An Exploration of General Social Survey Discussion Name Generator in a Chinese Context," *Social Networks* 20 (1998): 247–264.

27. Marsden, "Core Discussion Networks of Americans." Note that respondents to the GSS were allowed to name more than five alters, so that this set of density statistics is not strictly comparable with the results of our sociometric survey, which limited the maximum to five. However, given that only 4 percent of respondents named more than five alters, we can still use the GSS measure of density as a basis of a rough-and-ready comparison. Note also that the GSS distinguished "strong" and "weak" ties, and we do not. Marsden also discusses how density was calculated taking strength into account.

28. Marsden, "Core Discussion Networks of Americans."

29. Marsden, "Core Discussion Networks of Americans."

30. Marsden, "Core Discussion Networks of Americans."

31. Marsden, "Core Discussion Networks of Americans."

32. Marsden, "Core Discussion Networks of Americans."

33. Claude Fischer, *To Dwell Among Friends: Personal Networks in Town and City* (Chicago: University of Chicago Press, 1982), pp. 125–126. Marsden, "Core Discussion Networks of Americans," p. 125.

34. Sutcliffe and Bunderson, "Management Team Learning and Business Unit Performance."

35. For example, most networks uncovered by the GSS study were small, closed, and homogeneous. See, for example, Peter V. Marsden, "Homogeneity in Confiding Relations," *Social Networks* 10 (1988): 57–76, and Marsden, "Core Discussion Networks of Americans."

36. Marsden, "Core Discussion Networks of Americans."

37. Based on my analysis of the World Values Surveys, reported in Wayne E. Baker, "North Star Falling: The American Crisis of Values at the New Millennium," (unpublished manuscript, University of Michigan Business School, 1999).

38. Scott L. Feld, "The Focused Organization of Social Ties," *American Journal of Sociology* 86 (1981): 1015–1035.

39. Podolny and Baron, "Resources and Relationships."

40. Burt, *Structural Holes,* introduced and developed the concept of "structural holes" in egocentric networks. He champions the definition of social capital as an entrepreneurial network. Others define social capital as social closure. The two definitions of social capital are often pitted against each other. David Obstfeld and I argue that it is more productive to see these as different types of social capital, rather than to debate which one is "right"—see Wayne E. Baker and David Obstfeld, "Social Capital by Design: Structures, Strategies, and Institutional Context," in Leenders and Gabbay (eds.), *Corporate Social Capital and Liability,* chapter 4.

41. Podolny and Baron, "Resources and Relationships."

42. Marsden, "Homogeneity in Confiding Relations," and Marsden, "Core Discussion Networks of Americans."

43. Based on my analysis of the World Values Surveys, reported in Baker, "North Star Falling."

44. Podolny and Baron, "Resources and Relationships"; Baker and Obstfeld, "Social Capital by Design."

45. Ronald S. Burt, Joseph E. Jannotta, and James T. Mahoney, "Personality Correlates of Structural Holes," *Social Networks* 20 (1998): 63–87.

46. The authors of this study (referenced in Note 45) note that their conclusions are tentative, and provide four cautions about their interpretation of their results (see pp. 82–85). However, their findings are consistent

with the results from a long line of personality research on entrepreneurs: There is as much variation in personality among entrepreneurs as between entrepreneurs and nonentrepreneurs (see our summary in Baker and Obstfeld, "Social Capital by Design").

Chapter Three

1. This work involved using the Web-administered HUMAX Assessment (http://www.HUMAXnetworks.com). If I add paper-and-pencil methods, the total could be more than two thousand.
2. Lillian Too, *Feng Shui Fundamentals: Networking* (Shaftesbury, Dorset, Great Britain: Element Books, 1997).
3. Donna Fisher and Sandy Vilas, *Power Networking* (Austin, Tex.: MountainHarbour, 1996), pp. 27–28.
4. Robert B. Cialdini, *Influence: The Psychology of Persuasion* (New York: Morrow, 1993).
5. Cialdini, *Influence,* pp. 173–174.
6. See chapter 5 in Cialdini, *Influence.*
7. Wayne E. Baker and Robert R. Faulkner, "Diffusion of Fraud in the Capital Markets," paper presented at the annual meeting of the American Society of Criminology, Toronto (November 1999). We have presented earlier versions of this paper at the annual meeting of the International Network of Social Network Analysts (the "White Tie" event held in honor of Harrison C. White), as well as Wharton, University of Michigan, and other university venues.
8. Chapter 6 in Cialdini, *Influence.*
9. See chapter 11 in Wayne E. Baker, *Networking Smart* (New York: McGraw-Hill, 1994). There are over four thousand empirical studies of how information, ideas, products, and services spread or "diffuse" through networks. See Everett M. Rogers, *Diffusion of Innovations,* 4th ed. (New York: Free Press, 1995).
10. Fisher and Vilas, *Power Networking* (p. 21), describe those who do such things as "networking mongrels," people who "use and abuse networking."

11. For example, see Jean Baker Miller and Irene Pierce Stiver, *The Healing Connection* (Boston: Beacon Press, 1997); Joyce K. Fletcher, "Relational Practice," *Journal of Management Inquiry* 7 (1998): 163–186; Joyce K. Fletcher, "Developing an Interactive Self," *Social Policy* (summer, 1998): 48–51; Edward M. Hallowell, *Connect: Twelve Vital Ties That Open Your Heart, Lengthen Your Life, and Deepen Your Soul* (New York: Pantheon Books, 1999).

12. Barton J. Hirsch, "Social Networks and the Coping Process: Creating Personal Communities," in *Social Networks and Social Support,* edited by Benjamin H. Gottlieb, (Thousand Oaks, Calif.: Sage, 1981), pp. 149–170, quote from p. 169.

13. According to the Oracle, "Table of Bacon Numbers," as of December 28, 1999.

14. According to the Oracle, "The Center of the Hollywood Universe" (data compiled by the Oracle as of July 31, 1999). The most peripheral (obscure) actor in Hollywood (unnamed by a polite Oracle) has an average "number" of about 9. On Rod Steiger, visit the Oracle or see Duncan J. Watts, *Small Worlds* (Princeton, N.J.: Princeton University Press, 1999), p. 145. As the database grows, the structure changes, so actors and actresses may move up or down in the centrality rankings.

15. For an introduction to Erdös Numbers and access to the data, visit Professor Jerrold W. Grossman's Web site at Oakland University (http://www.oakland.edu/~grossman/).

16. From chapter 1, Paul Hoffman, *The Man Who Loved Only Numbers: The Story of Paul Erdös and the Search for Mathematical Truth* (New York: Hyperion, 1998,) via Hoffman's site at http://www.paulerdos.com/e2.html.

17. Malcolm Gladwell, "Six Degrees of Lois Weisberg," *New Yorker* (January 11, 1999): 53–63.

18. Gladwell, "Six Degrees of Lois Weisberg," p. 58.

19. Watts, *Small Worlds,* p. 4.

20. See Baker, *Networking Smart,* pp. 43–44, for a discussion of network size. For the calculation of two degrees of separation, see Ithiel de Sola Pool and Manfred Kochen, "Contacts and Influence," *Social Networks* 1 (1978/79): 5–51.

21. Scott L. Feld, "The Focused Organization of Social Ties," *American Journal of Sociology* 86 (1981): 1015–1035, quote on p. 1016.
22. In Baker, *Networking Smart,* pp. 41–42, I argue that the "similarity principle" is one of the five fundamental networking principles. It is well documented in social science research.
23. Mark Granovetter, "The Strength of Weak Ties," *American Journal of Sociology* 83 (1973): 1287–1303.
24. Watts, *Small Worlds,* p. 142. Watts introduces the terms *linchpins* and *shortcuts* (which he calls "short cuts") and provides their mathematical definitions.
25. Gladwell, "Six Degrees of Lois Weisberg," p. 54.
26. Based on research by Jerry Davis, which he provided to me in his class teaching notes, as well as his articles, such as Gerald F. Davis, "Agents without Principles? The Spread of the Poison Pill through the Intercorporate Network," *Administrative Science Quarterly* 36 (1991): 583–613, and Gerald F. Davis and Henrich R. Greve, "Corporate Elite Networks and Governance Changes in the 1980s," *American Journal of Sociology* 103 (1997): 1–37.
27. Duncan J. Watts, "Networks, Dynamics, and the Small-World Phenomenon," *American Journal of Sociology* 105 (1999): 493–527; Watts, *Small Worlds.*
28. Hallowell, *Connect,* pp. xiv–xv.
29. Joan O'C. Hamilton, "How to Talk the Talk," *Business Week* (September 27, 1999) EB92.
30. Wayne E. Baker and Gerald Davis, "Melissa McQwire" teaching case, University of Michigan Business School, 1999.
31. Erik Larson, "Free Money," *New Yorker* (October 11, 1999): 76–82.
32. Reported on the NEF's Web site, http://nef.bizserve.com.
33. Mission statement and details from the IT Zone Web site, http://www.annarboritzone.org.
34. Hirsch, "Social Networks and the Coping Process," p. 169.
35. Hirsch, "Social Networks and the Coping Process," pp. 156–160.
36. From materials supplied to me by Robert Pasick, Ph.D.
37. Jay Anand, "How Many Marriages Are Made in Heaven?" in the "Mastering Strategy" supplement to the *Financial Times* (October 25, 1999): 6–7.

38. Feld, "The Focused Organization of Social Ties," p. 1016.

39. Rosabeth Moss Kanter, "The Middle Manager as Innovator," *Harvard Business Review* (July-August, 1982): 95–105. See also "the power of peers" in Baker, *Networking Smart,* pp. 94–97.

40. Jeffrey Pfeffer, *Managing with Power* (Boston: Harvard Business School Press, 1992), p. 121.

41. Based on interview with Roberta Zald and her written summary of her job responsibilities.

42. Aimee Arlington and Wayne E. Baker, "Serving Two (or More) Masters: The Challenge and Promise of Multiple Accountabilities," in *Pressing Problems in Modern Organizations,* edited by Robert E. Quinn, Regina M. O'Neill, and Lynda St. Clair (New York: AMACOM, 2000), chapter 2.

43. Pyrra Alnot and Mary Yoko Brannen, "Cultural Misunderstanding: Effective Communication in Globally Diverse Organizations," in Quinn, O'Neill, and St. Clair, *Pressing Problems in Modern Organizations,* chapter 5.

44. Described in Wayne E. Baker, "The Paradox of Empowerment," *Chief Executive* 93 (April 1994): 62–65.

45. The story of Xerox's black caucus groups is told in several places, including chapter 7 of my *Networking Smart,* several Harvard Business School teaching cases, and research conducted by Raymond Friedman of Vanderbilt University.

46. See, for example, Paul S. Goodman and Eric D. Darr, "Computer-Aided Systems and Communities: Mechanisms for Organizational Learning in Distributed Environments," *MIS Quarterly* (December 1998): 417–440.

47. On communities of practice, see Jeffrey A. Martin and Paul R. Carlile, "Designing Agile Organizations: Organizational Learning at the Boundaries," in Quinn, O'Neill, and St. Clair, *Pressing Problems in Modern Organizations,* chapter 7.

48. Martin and Carlile, "Designing Agile Organizations."

49. For a demonstration, visit the IKNOW Web site at the University of Illinois, Champaign-Urbana, http://iknow.spcomm.uiuc.edu. For a published description, see Noshir Contractor, Dan Zink, and Michael Chan, "IKNOW: A Tool to Assist and Study the Creation, Maintenance, and Dissolution of Knowledge Networks," in *Community Computing*

·*and Support Systems, Lecture Notes in Computer Science 1519,*
edited by Toru Ishida (Berlin: Springer-Verlag, 1998), pp. 201–217.

50. Anjali Sastry and Fiona Lee, "Pairing Stability with Change: Rules, Operations, and Structures in an Enduring Organization," working paper, University of Michigan Business School, 2000.

51. Jean M. Bartunek and others, "A Group Mentoring Journey into the Department Chair Role," *Journal of Management Inquiry* 6 (1997): 270–279.

Chapter Four

1. Wayne E. Baker and David Obstfeld, "Social Capital by Design: Structures, Strategies, and Institutional Context," in *Corporate Social Capital and Liability,* edited by Roger Th. A. J. Leenders and Shaul M. Gabbay (Norwell, Mass.: Kluwer, 1999), chapter 4.

2. Robert B. Cialdini, *Influence: The Psychology of Persuasion* (New York: Morrow, 1993), pp. 18–19. I learned of this example of international reciprocity from this book. I have added some of the historical details.

3. Wilton S. Dillon, *Gifts and Nations* (The Hague, Netherlands: Mouton, 1969).

4. Robert Cialdini, "Instant Influence" (audiotape) (Palm Beach Gardens, Fla.: Dartnell, 1995).

5. Jeffrey Pfeffer and Robert I. Sutton, *The Knowing-Doing Gap* (Boston: Harvard Business School Press, 2000), chapter 7 (especially pp. 216–217). Pfeffer and Sutton base their description and analysis of BP largely on two cases written by Joel Podolny, John Roberts, and Andris Berzins, "British Petroleum: Performance and Growth (A)," Case S-1B-16A (Stanford, Calif.: Graduate School of Business, Stanford University, 1998), and "British Petroleum: Focus on Learning (B)," Case S-1B-16B (Stanford, Calif.: Graduate School of Business, Stanford University, 1998).

6. Alvin W. Gouldner, "The Norm of Reciprocity," *American Journal of Sociology* 25 (1960): 161–178; Alvin W. Gouldner, "Reciprocity and Autonomy in Functional Theory," in *Symposium on Sociological Theory,* edited by Llewellyn Gross (Evanston, Ill.: Row, Peterson, 1959),

pp. 241–270; Claude Levi-Strauss, "The Principle of Reciprocity," in *The Gift: An Interdisciplinary Perspective,* edited by Aafke E. Komter (Amsterdam: Amsterdam University Press, 1996), pp. 15–26; originally published 1949.

7. For example, see Levi-Strauss, "The Principle of Reciprocity"; Cialdini, "Reciprocation," chapter 2 in *Influence*; Paul DiMaggio, "Culture and Economy," chapter 2 in Neil J. Smelser and Richard Swedberg (eds.), *The Handbook of Economic Sociology* (Princeton: Princeton University Press, 1994); M. Lonkila, "Informal Exchange Relations in Post-Soviet Russia: A Comparative Perspective," *Sociological Research Online* 2 (1997): http://www.socresonline.org.uk/socresonline/2/2/9.html; Theodore Caplow, "Christmas Gifts and Kin Networks," *American Sociological Review* 47 (1982):383–392. See also Marcel Mauss, *The Gift* (translated by I. G. Cunnison) (London: Cohen and West, 1954); Bronislaw Malinowski, "The Principle of Give and Take," in *Crime and Custom in Savage Society* (London: Routledge and Kegan Paul, 1970), chapter 1, originally published 1922.

8. From Richard Leakey and R. Lewin, *People of the Lake* (New York: Doubleday, 1978). Quoted in Cialdini, *Influence,* p. 18. Similarly, sociologist Howard S. Becker argues that humans should be called *"Homo reciprocus."* See his *Man in Reciprocity* (New York: Praeger, 1956), p. 1.

9. Charles Darwin, *The Descent of Man* vol. 1 (Princeton, N.J.: Princeton University Press, 1981), originally published 1871. See pp. 163–164.

10. Becker, *Man in Reciprocity,* 1.

11. From Malinowski, *Crime and Custom in Savage Society,* quoted in Gouldner, "Reciprocity and Autonomy in Functional Theory," p. 267, f.n. 18.

12. From L. Tiger and R. Fox, *The Imperial Animal* (New York: Holt, Rinehart & Winston, 1971), quoted in Cialdini, *Influence,* p. 18.

13. Cialdini, *Influence,* p. 18.

14. See especially, Cialdini, *Influence,* pp. 30–36.

15. Cialdini, *Influence,* reviews several psychological experiments in chapter 2, "Reciprocation." The field of social exchange theory in sociology focuses on systems of two-party exchanges. Social exchange theory and network theory are natural partners; the combination has

produced a plethora of research. See, for example, David Willer (ed.), *Network Exchange Theory* (Westport, Conn.: Praeger, 1999).

16. These examples are summarized from chapter 2, "Reciprocation," in Cialdini, *Influence.*

17. See, especially, Cialdini, *Influence,* pp. 36–51.

18. Viktor E. Frankl, *The Will to Meaning* (New York: Meridian, 1988), p. 34 (italics added). Originally published 1970.

19. This figure was inspired by Frankl's graph of the indirect route to happiness, figure 3 (Frankl, *The Will to Meaning,* p. 34).

20. Frankl, *The Will to Meaning,* p. 35. Italics in original.

21. On the concept of generalized reciprocity, see, for example, Nobuyuki Takahashi, "The Emergence of Generalized Exchange," *American Journal of Sociology* 105 (2000): 1105–1134. This research shows that generalized reciprocity can emerge among self-interested egoists in the absence of collective norms.

22. For example, Cialdini suggests the use of this tactic in his audiotape *Instant Influence.* In my opinion, his advice here is short-sighted.

23. For exercises related to active listening, see, for example, J. William Pfeiffer and John E. Jones, *A Handbook of Structured Experiences for Human Relations Training* vol. 1 (San Francisco: Jossey-Bass, 1974); Robert E. Quinn and others, *Becoming a Master Manager* (New York: Wiley, 1996), pp. 48–50.

24. Stephen R. Covey, *The Seven Habits of Highly Effective People* (New York: Simon & Schuster, 1989), p. 240.

25. Covey, *The Seven Habits of Highly Effective People,* p. 240.

26. Wayne E. Baker, "The Paradox of Empowerment," *Chief Executive* 93 (April 1994): 62–65.

27. From Edward M. Hallowell, *Connect: Twelve Vital Ties That Open Your Heart, Lengthen Your Life, and Deepen Your Soul* (New York: Pantheon Books, 1999), pp. 124–126.

28. Lee Sproull and Sara Kiesler, *Connections* (Cambridge, Mass.: MIT Press, 1992). See chapter 5 for a discussion of how electronic communication can increase personal connections for isolated or peripheral people.

29. Barry Wellman and Keith Hampton, "Living Networked On and Offline," *Contemporary Sociology* 28 (1999): 648–654.

30. Sproull and Kiesler, *Connections,* p. 39.

31. For example, see Gary M. Olson and Judith S. Olson, "Distance Matters," working paper, University of Michigan, School of Information, 1999.

32. Based on e-mail message from my colleague, professor Judy Olson, University of Michigan Business School (October 28, 1999).

33. Based on e-mail message from my colleague, Professor Judy Olson, University of Michigan Business School (October 28, 1999).

34. Hallowell describes several such business episodes in chapter 11 of *Connect.*

35. Jon Kjos kindly gave me a copy of the guide, called "To Manner Born/To Manners Bred: A Hip-Pocket Guide to Etiquette for the Hampden-Sydney Man." The version I have was published in 1990 by the Office of the Dean of Students, Hampden-Sydney College.

36. Susan RoAne, *The Secrets of Savvy Networking* (New York: Time Warner, 1993), p. 169.

37. I am grateful to 2000 MBA student Chris Workman for bringing this example to my attention.

38. Brian Uzzi, "The Sources and Consequences of Embeddedness for the Economic Performance of Organizations: The Network Effect," *American Sociological Review* 61 (1996): 674–698. Quote from p. 679.

39. Baker, *Networking Smart,* pp. 57–58.

40. John E. Tropman, *Making Meetings Work* (Thousand Oaks, Calif.: Sage, 1996).

41. Robert Slater, *The GE Way Fieldbook* (New York: McGraw-Hill, 2000), p. 64.

42. See Table 1 in Peter V. Marsden and Elizabeth H. Gorman, "Social Capital in Internal Staffing Practices," in *Corporate Social Capital and Liability,* edited by Roger Th. A. J. Leenders and Shaul M. Gabbay (Norwell, Mass.: Kluwer, 1999), chapter 10, p. 188.

43. R. A. Burgelman, "Intraorganizational Ecology of Strategy Making and Organizational Adaptation: Theory and Field Research," *Organization Science* 2 (1991): 239–262. For other examples, see M. D. Hutt, H. Reingen, and J. R. Rochetto Jr., "Tracing Emergent Processes in Marketing Strategy Formation," *Journal of Marketing* 52 (1988): 4–19.

44. Rosabeth Moss Kanter, *The Change Masters* (New York: Simon & Schuster, 1983), p. 141.
45. Ron Ashkenas, Dave Ulrich, Todd Jick, and Steve Kerr, *The Boundaryless Organization: Breaking the Chains of Organizational Structure* (San Francisco: Jossey-Bass, 1995), pp. 17–18.
46. Quoted in Ram Charan and Noel M. Tichy, *Every Business Is a Growth Business* (New York: Times Business, 1998), p. 299.
47. J. A. Starr and I. C. MacMillan, "Resource Cooptation Via Social Contracting: Resource Acquisition Strategies for New Ventures," *Strategic Management Journal* 11 (1990): 79–92. Quote from p. 86.
48. Baker, "The Paradox of Empowerment."
49. Charan and Tichy, *Every Business Is a Growth Business,* p. 313.
50. Harry V. Roberts and Bernard F. Sergesketter, *Quality Is Personal* (New York: Free Press, 1993). On page xi, they describe how they met. My description of the personal quality checklist and its use is based on this book, but I have adapted the concept for networking purposes.
51. Roberts and Sergesketter, *Quality Is Personal,* p. 9.
52. Roberts and Sergesketter, *Quality Is Personal,* p. 30.
53. Roberts and Sergesketter, *Quality Is Personal,* p. 38.
54. Roberts and Sergesketter, *Quality Is Personal,* p. 29.
55. Donna Fisher and Sandy Vilas, *Power Networking* (Austin, Tex.: MountainHarbour, 1992). Quote on p. 28; see also pp. 124, 142, 163–164.
56. Fisher and Vilas, *Power Networking,* p. 133.
57. Reported in Peter J. Frost, Jane E. Dutton, Monica C. Worline, and Annette Wilson, "Narratives of Compassion in Organizations," in *Emotion in Organizations,* edited by Stephen Fineman (Thousand Oaks, Calif.: Sage, 2000).
58. Described in Jon Birger, "Women in Business: Creating a New Girls Club," *Crain's New York Business* (September 29, 1997): 17.

Chapter Five

1. Jeffrey Pfeffer, *The Human Equation* (Boston: Harvard Business School Press, 1998). Chapter 1, "Looking for Success in All the Wrong Places," summarizes his argument.

2. Pfeffer, *The Human Equation,* p. 5.

3. Ram Charan and Noel M. Tichy, *Every Business a Growth Engine* (New York: Times Business/Random House, 1999), p. 296. Italics added.

4. This section is based on, and adapted from, Wayne E. Baker, "The Paradox of Empowerment," *Chief Executive* 93 (April 1994): 62–65.

5. For an analysis of the dysfunctional consequences of this philosophy, see, for example, Robert E. Lane, "Work as 'Disutility' and Money as 'Happiness': Cultural Origins of a Basic Market Error," *Journal of Socio-Economics* 21 (1992): 43–64.

6. Douglas McGregor, *The Human Side of Enterprise* (New York: Mc-Graw-Hill, 1985), p. 37. Originally published 1960. On managers' fears of natural "groupiness" (or, what I call networks), see pp. 37–38.

7. I first used the term "conditions of interaction" in "The Paradox of Empowerment."

8. Leon Festinger, Stanley Schachter, and Kurt Back, *Social Pressures in Informal Groups: A Study of Human Factors in Housing* (Stanford, Calif.: Stanford University Press, 1950). Jerry Davis kindly supplied me with his summary of this study. This is Jerry's favorite example of the relationship between architecture and social networks; it's come to be my favorite, too.

9. Festinger, Schachter, and Back, *Social Pressures in Informal Groups,* p. 37.

10. Festinger, Schachter, and Back, *Social Pressures in Informal Groups,* p. 10.

11. Scott L. Feld, "The Focused Organization of Social Ties," *American Journal of Sociology* 86 (1981): 1015–1035.

12. See, for example, Helena Z. Lopata and David Maines (eds.), *Friendship in Context* (Greenwich, Conn.: JAI Press, 1988). Malcolm Gladwell discusses this point in his "Six Degrees of Lois Weisberg," *New Yorker* (January 11, 1999): 53–63.

13. Gladwell, "Six Degrees of Lois Weisberg," p. 56.

14. Peter M. Blau and Joseph Schwartz, *Cross-Cutting Social Circles* (New York: Academic Press, 1984). For related research, see Matthijs Kalmijn, "Status Homogamy in the United States," *American Journal of Sociology* 97 (1991): 496–523.

15. Festinger, Schachter, and Back, *Social Pressures in Informal Groups,* p. 11.

16. This is a huge, multidisciplinary literature. A small sample will indicate its diversity: Leon Festinger, Stanley Schachter, and Kurt Back, "Architecture and Group Membership," *Journal of Social Issues* 7 (1951): 152–163; R. B. Blake and others, "Housing Architecture and Social Interaction," *Sociometry* 19 (1956): 133–139; S. Mazumdar, "How Birds of a Feather Flock Together in Organizations: The Phenomenon of Sociophysical Congregation and Distancing," *Journal of Architectural Planning Research* 12 (1995): 1–18; B.W.P. Wells, "The Psycho-social Influence of Building Environment: Sociometric Findings in Large and Small Office Spaces," *Building Science* 1 (1965): 153–165; Christophe Van de Bulte and Rudy K. Moenaert, "The Effects of R&D Team Co-location on Communication Patterns among R&D, Marketing, and Manufacturing," *Management Science* 44 (1998): S1-S18; Gary M. Olson and Judith S. Olson, "Distance Matters," working paper, University of Michigan, School of Information, 1999.

17. James S. Coleman, *Foundations of Social Theory* (Cambridge, Mass.: Harvard University Press, 1990), p. 300.

18. Karl E. Weick, *Sensemaking in Organizations* (Thousand Oaks, Calif.: Sage, 1995), p. 87.

19. Feld, "The Focused Organization of Social Ties," 1016.

20. Howard Aldrich, *Organizations Evolving* (Thousand Oaks, Calif.: Sage, 1999), pp. 147–148.

21. From an e-mail message Aundrea Almond-Wallace sent to me on November 1, 1999.

22. Wayne E. Baker, "Capital Partners" (1990, p. 8) and "Capital Partners—1996" (1996). Teaching cases, University of Michigan Business School.

23. Alun Anderson, "A Unique Labor Design Fits the British to a Tea," *Science* 2 (July 1991): 377–378. Quoted in Baker, *Networking Smart,* p. 134.

24. David A. Nalder and Michael L. Tushman, *Competing by Design: The Power of Organizational Architecture* (New York: Oxford University Press, 1997), p. 9.

25. Jon R. Katzenbach and Douglas K. Smith, *The Wisdom of Teams* (Boston: Harvard Business School Press, 1993), p. 45.

26. Nancy Tennant Snyder and Deborah Duarte, "Chaotic Role Movement in Large Organizations: From Planning to Dynamic Management," in *Pressing Problems in Modern Organizations,* edited by Robert E. Quinn, Regina M. O'Neill, and Lynda St. Clair (New York: AMACOM, 2000), chapter 6.

27. Snyder and Duarte, "Chaotic Role Movement in Large Organizations," p. 113.

28. Snyder and Duarte, "Chaotic Role Movement in Large Organizations," p. 113.

29. See, for example, chapter 15 in Baker, *Networking Smart;* Robert Slater, *The GE Way Fieldbook* (New York: McGraw-Hill, 2000), p. 64.

30. Slater, *The GE Way Fieldbook,* p. 149.

31. Statistics from F. Brian Talbot and B. Joseph White, "Winning Hearts and Minds with Education," Mastering Strategy Series, *Financial Times* (September 27, 1999).

32. Talbot and White, "Winning Hearts and Minds with Education."

33. See discussion in Aldrich, *Organizations Evolving,* pp. 143–144.

34. See, for example, Paul S. Goodman and Eric D. Darr "Computer-Aided Systems and Communities: Mechanisms for Organizational Learning in Distributed Environments," *MIS Quarterly* (December 1998): 417–440.

35. Noah Barsky, "A Core/Periphery Structure in a Corporate Budgeting Process," *Connections* 22 (1999): 28–51; S. F. Jablonsky and Noah Barsky, "Integrating Strategy, Control and Accountability," *Corporate Finance Review* 4 (1999): 27–35; S. F. Jablonsky, J. Keating, and J. B. Heian, *Business Advocate or Corporate Policeman? Assessing Your Role as a Financial Executive* (Morristown, N.J.: Financial Executives Research Foundation, 1993).

36. Jablonsky and Barsky, "Integrating Strategy, Control and Accountability," p. 28.

37. Ram Charan, "How Networks Reshape Organizations for Results," *Harvard Business Review* (September-October 1991): 104–115.

38. Slater, *The GE Way Fieldbook,* pp. 82–83.

39. Jack Maple, with Chris Mitchell, *The Crime Fighter* (New York: Doubleday, 1999).

40. Matthew Fordahl, "Still No Word from Mars," Associated Press (December 5, 1999).

41. Toby E. Stuart, "Alliance Networks: View from the Hub," Mastering Strategy Series, *Financial Times* (November 15, 1999).

42. Steve Kerr, "On the Folly of Rewarding A While Hoping for B," *Academy of Management Journal* 18 (1975): 769–783.

43. Wayne E. Baker and Robert R. Faulkner, "The Social Organization of Conspiracy: Illegal Networks in the Heavy Electrical Equipment Industry," *American Sociological Review* 58 (1993): 837–860.

44. National Public Radio, *All Things Considered* (December 8, 1999). Available on NPR Web site, http://www.npr.org.

45. Wayne E. Baker, "The Network Organization in Theory and Practice," in *Networks and Organizations: Structure, Form, and Action,* edited by N. Nohria and R. G. Eccles (Boston: Harvard Business School Press, 1992), chapter 15. Quote on p. 398.

Additional Resources

■ Assessment Tool

- The HUMAX Assessment of Social Capital

  This is the most advanced and comprehensive sociometric survey of social capital available. It is administered entirely via the Web. The service is available around the globe twenty-four hours a day, seven days a week. After the user completes the online survey, immediate feedback is provided online in a twenty-four-page customized report. This report includes a network diagram, social capital profile type, and an analysis of three dimensions of social capital. If taken as part of a group or organization, it also provides each user with a detailed composite report, including the distribution of profile types in the group or organization. Both reports can be printed or downloaded.

  For more information, visit the HUMAX Corporation Web site at http://www.HUMAXnetworks.com. A fee is charged for use; group rates available. This site also includes free downloadable articles on networks and social capital (click "Articles" on the menu bar).

■ Books

- Wayne E. Baker, *Networking Smart: How to Build Relationships for Personal and Organizational Success.* New York: McGraw-Hill, 1994. (Reprinted 2000 by Backinprint.com. Available through major online booksellers.)

Fifteen chapters on all aspects of networks. The book is divided into four parts: The Networking Perspective (three chapters), Managing Relationships and Networks Inside the Organization (five chapters), Managing Relationships and Networks Outside the Organization (six chapters), and Conclusion (one chapter). *Networking Smart* is a business best-seller. Named one of the top thirty business books of the year by Executive Book Summaries, *Networking Smart* was a main selection of the Business Week and Newbridge Book Clubs.

- Ron Burt, *Structural Holes: The Social Structure of Competition.* Cambridge, Mass.: Harvard University Press, 1992.

A classic, pioneering study of social capital in large organizations. *Structural Holes* includes chapters on concepts and measurement, an analysis of a population of managers that shows the relationship between social capital and promotion, and an analysis of firms in various industries that shows the relationship between an organization's social capital and profits. Some chapters are very technical.

- Robert D. Putnam, *Bowling Alone: The Collapse and Revival of American Community.* New York: Simon & Schuster, 2000.

A comprehensive analysis of trends in civic engagement and social capital in America. It argues that Americans have become increasingly disconnected over the past twenty-five years. It documents the benefits of social capital for education, safe neighborhoods, economic prosperity, health, happiness, and democracy, and offers a prescription for rebuilding American social capital.

- Roger Th. A. J. Leenders and Shaul M. Gabbay (eds.), *Corporate Social Capital and Liability.* Norwell, Mass.: Kluwer, 1999.

Twenty-five chapters by an international group of experts in social networks and social capital. Includes conceptual issues (theory, models, and management), structure at the individual level (social capital in jobs and careers; social capital and management), and structure at the firm level (social capital in collaboration and alliances; social capital and financial capital).

- Stanley Wasserman and Katherine Faust, *Social Network Analysis: Methods and Applications.* Cambridge, England: Cambridge University Press, 1994.

An excellent introduction to the statistics and methods of network analysis. Very technical. It includes mathematical representations of social networks, graphs and matrices, structural and locational properties, various measures of roles and positions, dyadic and triadic methods, and statistical dyadic interaction.

■ Organization

- International Network for Social Network Analysis (INSNA)

INSNA is a nonprofit professional association "for researchers interested in social network analysis."

It publishes *Connections,* which contains news, articles, technical columns, abstracts, and book reviews; sponsors the annual International Social Networks Conference; maintains electronic services such as SOCNET, an electronic discussion forum; keeps a database of information on members; and has links to various reference sources and related home pages. For more information or to join the association, visit INSNA's Web site at http://www.heinz.cmu.edu/project/INSNA/.

The Author

Wayne Baker is professor of organizational behavior and human resource management and director of the Center for Society & Economy at the University of Michigan Business School. He is a faculty associate at the University of Michigan Institute for Social Research.

Baker is director of research at HUMAX Corporation, an assessment and training firm specializing in personal and organizational development (http://www.HUMAXnetworks.com). At HUMAX, he led the development of the Web-administered HUMAX Assessment of Social Capital, as well as the firm's Achieving Success Through Social Capital training workshop. He has also consulted to, and conducted executive training for, many major corporations, associations, financial institutions, and professional service firms.

He teaches courses on organizational behavior, networks and social capital, organizational design, and general management in the University of Michigan Business School's programs: Executive Education, Ph.D., MBA, and BBA. Baker has won both the Emory Williams Award for Excellence in Teaching and the Max Weber Award for Distinguished Scholarship.

Baker's interests include social capital, networks, innovative management practices, economic sociology, and culture. His business best-seller *Networking Smart: How to Build Relationships for Personal and Organizational Success* (McGraw-Hill, 1994) was a main selection in the Newbridge Book Club, the Business Week Book Club, and Executive Book Summaries (EBS). EBS named *Networking Smart* "one of the top 30 business books" of the year.

His research has been published in the *American Sociological Review, American Journal of Sociology, California Management Review, Chief Executive, Training Today, American Behavioral Scientist, Journal of Mathematical Sociology, Connections*, and elsewhere.

Prior to joining the University of Michigan faculty in 1995, he was on the faculty at the University of Chicago Graduate School of Business. Earlier, he was a postdoctoral research fellow in organizational behavior and finance at Harvard Business School, and a partner and senior manager of TSG, a Washington, D.C.–based management consulting firm.

In 1981 he earned his Ph.D. in sociology from Northwestern University. He has an M.A. in sociology (1976) and a B.S. in finance, summa cum laude (1974), from Northern Illinois University.

Index